infoChina

The complete t...

...uide

BEIJING

P.T. Smallbone.

Tourist Publications

Published in the United Kingdom by
T P Books & Print Ltd
11a East Street
Leighton Buzzard
Bedfordshire LU7 8HU
United Kingdom
In association with
Tourist Publications
6 Piliou Street
Koliatsou Square
112 55 Athens

Copyright © Tourist Publications 1989

Produced by
T P Books & Print Ltd
in Australia

Editorial Directors:	L. Starr, Y. Skordilis
Typography:	Deblaere Typeseting Pty Ltd
Layout:	Bookcraft Pty Ltd
Photo-setting:	Deblaere Typesetting Pty Ltd
Authors:	B. Howie
	N. Bliss
Photographs:	William Torrens Pty Ltd
Colour Separations:	Chroma Graphics
Maps:	Lovell Johns Ltd

Printed in Singapore

ISBN 960 7587 15 4

Due to the wealth of information available it has been necessary
to be selective. Sufficient detail is given to allow the visitor to
make choices depending on personal taste, and the information
has been carefully checked. However, errors creep in an
changes will occur. We hope you will forgive the errors and
omissions and find this book a helpful companion.

ABOUT THIS GUIDE

Come and see Beijing, The capital, The seat of power, The home of the 'Body corporate'. Enjoy the food, the mythology, the scenery and fall in love with Beijing like we have.

This guide offers all that you need. Part I gives general information about Beijing, including history, culture, government, geology, climate, flora, fauna etc.

Part II offers conveniently described sightseeing both in and out of the city, arranged for both a casual tour or a more detailed inspection, you pick what you want.

Part III consists of a full accommodation listing with useful additional information.

Part IV is full of practical information, starting before you arrive and taking you through shopping and eating, getting around and a page or two for 'Help!'. Part V is a special section for business visitors.

Colour maps of China and the city of Beijing have been included. We hope you have a wonderful time in Beijing and that you will love our city as we do, honouring her virtues and forgiving her faults.

She is unique and special.

Table of Contents

PART I
General Introduction

CHINA AND HER PEOPLE

THE ENIGMA

The road from Beijing's international airport runs a long, straight course between groves of poplars and willows before ending in the confusion of downtown Beijing.

This is a simple metaphor for China today.

Up until the 1980's, whether trailing in the wake of the excesses of the various Imperial Courts or suffering the wretchedness of a Cultural Revolution, China and her people had always steered a straight course towards what they firmly believed was their ideological nirvana.

Today that straight course is heading for confusion as China, more boldly than other Eastern Bloc countries – but with less bureaucratic understanding – heads into the tricky world of capitalism.

Beijing, capital of the world's most populous socialist nation, is a prime example of a country torn between the reality of life in today's 20th. century and the ingrained beliefs of uncompromising Marxist doctrines.

On the one hand, as China's rulers flirt with the West, luxury, high-rise hotels are changing the drab Beijing skyline whilst at street level local youth takes to jeans and Coca Cola.

Yet on the other hand, the apartment blocks for the workers have the charm and atmosphere of a commune; the bureaucrats run rampant and the hard-line politicians mutter in their wispy beards about the wisdom of free enterprise.

This is the enigma of China! The ancient, the modern, the liberal and the doctrinaire each jostling for attention.

It is unlikely the average visitor will appreciate this – or, for that matter, really need to.

At most there will be a superficial feeling that Beijing is a strange mixture.

Coming from Shanghai or Guangzhou (Canton) the traveller immediately notices a faintly musty, old-fashioned air so unlike the slick, cosmopolitan 'virtues' of the southern cities. It's as though Beijing has forgotten to wind the alarm and is still snoozing away in an earlier decade.

But, for all the quaintness, there is still that buzz in the air. It is the capital. It is the seat of power. It is the home of the 'body corporate', the National People's Congress. And it is the last resting place of the nearest thing to a saint in the Chinese lexicon – Chairman Mao.

For Westerners the obvious attraction of Beijing and China is the attraction of forbidden fruit. The closure of the country's borders, in the wake of the Communist's rise to power after World War 11, sealed off the nation and its people from the unwanted and interfering gaze of the 'barbarians' of the outside world.

The West could only watch and wonder as reports filtered through the Bamboo Curtain chronicling dreadful tales of internal turmoil. Like the dragon of its ancient mythology China writhed and belched flame as new politics and old traditions met head on.

Gradually the dragon settled. If not content, at least inert.

Geology and Geography

China dominates Asia with her sheer bulk and geographical position. The third largest country in the world (after U.S.S.R. and Canada) China sprawls across 9,560,990 sq.kms.

Her borders encompass the Soviet Union, Mongolia, Afghanistan, India, Pakistan, Bhutan, Sikkim, Burma, Laos, Vietnam and North Korea.

But China is far from land-locked having 6,647 kms. of coastline along the Yellow, East China and South China seas.

Within her territory there is every kind of topographic condition: a glance at a map of China reveals a rough semi-circle of mountains acting as a natural barrier dividing the desolate mountain and desert regions of the Western two-thirds of the country from the coastal and semi-tropic regions of the remaining third in the East.

The **Northern part** of China is in thrall to the vast Gobi desert whose dunes reach towards the high, grassland plateaus of Inner Mongolia.

The **Southern part** extends from the spectacular, icy peaks of Tibet across to the monsoonal, humid flatlands and hills of the South-West and Hong Kong.

Bei hai Park

These geological variations give China a unique appeal but the very remoteness and the limited access of the interior will deter all but the most determined traveller.

Perseverance can be rewarding though and a latter-day Marco Polo could find himself in such singular areas as the **Xin Jiang** basin with its 'celestial mountains' peaking at over 4,000 freezing metres whilst, on the plateau below, the Tufan Depression sinks 150 metres below sea level with searing 47°C temperatures.

More readily accessible are the rare limestone formations of Guilin where, thanks to erosion, hundreds of strange formations arise out of the plains like a stone forest of some mythical monster's imagination.

Basically China can be described as a giant staircase dropping down in a series of graduated plateaus from the mountains of the west to the coastal plains of the east.

Beijing is at the 'foot' of these stairs.

The city was built on the edge of the North China Plain which had been formed by ancient alluvial deposits from the Yongding and Chaobai rivers. To the east, 113 kms. away, lies the Gulf of Bohai; to the north-east, the Yanshan Mountain range; and to the west are the Taihang mountains.

Beijing is far from compact. Taking advantage of its location the suburbs spread out 25 kms. towards the Western hills.

Climate and Temperature

As to be expected with a country of its size, China's climate runs the gamut from hot to cold with extremes producing little or no rain in the inland deserts but monsoonal downpours in the Tropic of Cancer regions in the south-east.

Beijing, located 39 56'N., 116 20''E and 44.38 metres above sea level, is subject to monsoonal winds. Warm, moist currents from the south-east in summer bring heavy rains to the capital, especially in July. In winter those winds swing round to the north-west and bring the chill of Siberia across the plains of Inner Mongolia.

The annual average temperature is 11.8°C., with January's average dropping to −4.7°C. whilst July reaches an average of 26.1°C. It is not unusual for winter temperatures to drop to −20°C. with an additional, severe wind chill factor.

The visitor sensitive to weather variations will probably find the short Autumn months of September and October the best time to travel although calm, windless days can produce a throat-searing pollution from the coal fires that generate much of the power for industrial use, and warmth and cooking for domestic use. If well rugged up I can recommend the clear, crisp days of late January and February.

Flora and Fauna

The popular image of China's flora and fauna can easily be summed up in the two words 'willow' and 'panda'. You will see plenty of the former but, with the exception of zoos, nothing of the latter.

With the vastness of China covering arid, temperate and sub-tropic climatic zones, the trees and shrubs reflect the different conditions.

The tourist will notice a number of familiar European names amongst the flora of the country. There are also regional varieties of orchids, oleanders, chrysanthemums, poppies and lotuses. Bamboo and teak trees abound and there is even a scattering of Australian eucalypts.

The Chinese are particularly fond of the tall poplars which they plant along the road verges giving the countryside a distinctly French look.

Crops and fruits are similarly diverse although there is a natural emphasis on regional produce such as rice, tea, sugar cane, pineapples, pomegranates and lychees.

As food needs are paramount, the Chinese cannot afford the luxury of growing flowers for their own sake. Any decorative blooms you may see in homes or hotels tend to be 'grown' from rare, plastic hybrids.

With fauna, China shares the same dilemma as the rest of the world with declining numbers of wild animals, most notably the **Giant Panda.** This cute, lumbering animal has fallen prey to both Man and Mother Nature. One uses the gun and the snare. The other uses the vagaries of climate to affect production of the special type of bamboo on which the Panda depends.

Other indigenous animals such as the **Golden Monkey** from Sichuan, the **Yangtze alligator** and the **Manchurian Tiger** are now mainly seen in zoos. The only native animal of any distinction in great numbers is the **Tibetan Yak.**

Bird fanciers are better catered for, although Beijing is very light in the sparrow department thanks to an ill-considered Government decision in the 1950's to wipe out all birds in the capital.

Nevertheless the Chinese have a passion for small singing birds and a popular Sunday pastime in Beijing is watching the old men gathering to gossip and listen to the songs of their tiny caged pets. It is tempting to speculate on the symbolism of this weekly ritual!

In the countryside the keen-eyed watcher can still spot such rarities as the **Manchurian Crane,** the **Asian Barred** owlet, the **Maribou Stork** and the **green peafowl.**

A surprising number of mangy moggies and lean-sided dogs prowl the outskirts of Beijing and the country villages. As they seem to serve no purpose either as pets or watchdogs one can only assume they will end up on the dinner table.

Welcome to China

Government

'Democracy means simply the bludgeoning of the people by the people for the people' (Oscar Wilde).

Wilde's cynical misquote of Abraham Lincoln's Gettysburg Address could well be applied to the unwieldy, centralised apparatus set up with the declaration of the Republic of China on 1st.October 1949.

Refinements and shifts in power and titles since then have altered the facade of the ruling bodies but China can't escape the fact that the politicians and the Army, keen to keep the power base in Beijing, have created a bureaucratic juggernaut that sporadically gets out of control and the country finds itself in the throes of an ill-conceived Great Leap Forward at best or a bloody, morale-shaking Cultural Revolution at worst.

Central to the control of China is the power of the Communist Party's Central Committee who determine the top jobs, the governing principles and the overall national policies of government.

The nominal law-making body is the National People's Congress consisting of elected deputies from the several hundred provinces of

China. The Standing Committee is the power-wielding organ of the Congress which acts as the legislative branch controlled by the Central Committee of the Communist Party.

Day-to-day housekeeping is done by the State Council answerable to both the National People's Congress and the Central Committee of the Communist Party. As the executive branch of government the State Council controls the general activities of the various ministries including Education, Public Security, Radio & Television, Culture and Defence.

Government then spirals down through the various provincial councils to the 'xian' or district. At the bottom of the pyramid are the communal 'danwais' or work units to which every worker belongs. The 'danwai' or commune as it is more readily recognised determines the very social existence of the worker with job transfers, marriage permission and even childbirth being governed at local level.

In theory all Chinese citizens over the age of eighteen can vote or stand for election but democracy ends there for the only opposition within the Government are any factional cliques.

The Chinese political system is forever evolving and recent attempts at liberal reform have tended to underline the cumbersome nature of the beast and the reactionary attitudes of many of the old time politicians.

Guard at Imperial Palace

Justice

Significant changes have been made to the administration of justice within China.

In the early days of the Revolution there appeared to be little difference between the ruthless, unquestioned power of the Emperors and the ruthless, unquestioned power of the Revolutionary Courts.

Latterly, however, a revised criminal code has made positive progress towards more humane judicial attitudes.

All citizens are officially considered equal before the law. Every accused person is entitled to legal defence and freedom from torture.

No doubt summary justice is still done especially at the commune level but a system of magistrates normally acting on panels rather than alone will hear major cases

The device of the 'show trial' is often used to make a political point (e.g. Gang of Four) or a moral lesson (e.g. murder and fraud trials).

In the case of serious crime, in which category economic crime ranks with murder, the death sentence will be imposed and carried out.

Generally though, prison terms with the emphasis on re-education rather than mere revenge punishment are handed out.

Tourists will often be surprised, as I was, to be shown over a model prison such as the Shanxi Provincial Prison No.1, outside Taiyuan. Here the governor pointed out that the stress was on reform and the 'three educations': political, cultural and technical. Work in the prison factories producing aluminium ware and plastic shoes was complemented with regular indoctrination sessions. Officials admitted to 'harsh treatment' for those who resisted attempts at reform.

To the casual eye law and order appears almost non-existent. Beijing's notorious cyclists blithely disregard traffic policemen's signals. Fights in the street are ignored except by the curious onlookers. Any official display seems reserved for official functions and visiting dignitaries who are whipped through the city in a frenzy of sirens and motorcades.

> **INFOTIP:** Tourists will feel thankfully safe in China and, despite an increase in minor pickpocketing, violence is rare.

Education

Surprisingly, despite a deserved reputation as a cultural and artistic giant, China's record for universal education has not been a proud one.

Under the Imperial dynastic regimes education was reserved for the ruling and middle classes. Neglect, deliberate or by default, left the masses in a state of literate subjugation.

After the 1949 proclamation of the Republic, and in line with the Communist philosophy of a carefully educated proletariat, the Chinese hierarchy instituted an educational system that was open to all, albeit compulsory.

The system corresponds roughly to that operating within Western countries: Nursery, Primary, Secondary and Tertiary.

The Nursery or Creche program is obviously of great importance for the successful creation of minds receptive to the formative political training which will intensify during the later years of education.

However there is more than just early indoctrination behind these kindergartens as the Chinese have a natural love of children and the care and encouragement they receive is a manifestation of that love.

Foreign visitors are welcome at the creches and also at the so-called 'Children's Palaces' which are extra-curricular schools for the brighter kiddies most of whom wear the red scarf denoting membership of the Young Pioneers, the junior branch of the Communist Party.

At the Children's Palace the tots get more advanced instruction in the arts including music, dancing, singing, craft modelling and even simple electronics. The skill and talent of the ankle-biters is simply awesome.

Generally speaking all young children attend a creche of some description as the mothers are usually in the workforce except in the later stages of pregnancy and for a period after the birth. Those too young for kindergarten are cared for by their grandmothers.

At the age of seven the children are sent to primary school until the age of thirteen. During these years there is a heavy concentration on the study of the Chinese language which is understandable considering there are 50,000 'pictographs' or characters in the language of which 5,000 are in common use. Eight major dialects can add further complications. From ten onwards the students will move into other languages mainly English, French or Russian.

Thirteen is the age when Chinese children move to a Secondary school where they face two degrees of education. The first degree will take them up to age sixteen when many will leave to get a job. Those who remain face a tougher second degree course preparatory to entering a tertiary institution. Secondary education puts a heavier emphasis on the sciences and very little on what we would call a liberal arts curriculum. Instruction is not restricted to school hours and students are expected to spend much of their free time in political classes and physical training.

At the end of their secondary years the students will undergo a school-leaving exam and shortly afterwards a competitive exam before graduating to higher education.

The bulk of students will finish one or both degrees of their secondary education. An elite will have the opportunity to go to university and with that opportunity the potential for a better job, a better lifestyle and overseas travel. The wheel has turned and whilst

Visiting a local school

the intellectual and the scientist were despised and humiliated during the unhappy days of the Cultural Revolution today they form the backbone of a new, pragmatic China.

Tertiary study becomes more intensive with most students living on the campus of one of the forty or so universities throughout the country with the main ones being Beijing, Shanghai, Nanking, Canton and Wuhan. Ironically Beijing's university had its origins in Yanjing University which had been set up by the United States from reparation money received after the Boxer Rebellion.

Not only are the students' days full but their after-hours are devoted to further political lectures, sports and a range of community activities including compulsory farm labouring.

A range of specialist institutes train pupils in traditional arts and crafts and there is even a Modern Language Institute which turns out translators at production line speed—they fill the desperate need for tour guides because of the burgeoning tourist industry and as interpreters for the business and political requirements of foreign trade.

The top graduates not only get the plum jobs in China but also the prized chance for post-graduate study overseas.

Technical training tends to be done on the job with factories providing on-site facilities with the student learning the manual skills during the day and furthering his mental education after hours.

The ordinary worker is also encouraged to study in his spare time with the help of local district classes and special education programs on radio and television.

Commerce and Industry

Despite the ingrained bureaucratic mistrust of the capitalist system a realistic approach to both domestic and international trade has produced a remarkable change to the business face of China.

This is most noticeable in the area of tourism which is enjoying boom times but at a price.

Trade and industry are progressing at a marginally slower pace and with fewer problems thanks to established, sophisticated trading practises that date from China's earliest days

The emergence of an entrepreneurial, private-enterprise approach to trade has been one of the more surprising developments. This has not been without some soul-searching and some heartburn as shrewd businessmen abuse the freedom they have unexpectedly won. China is faced with the surfacing of a new, wealthy class which sits uneasily beside the professed socialist purity of the country. The government has the difficult task of compromising beliefs in its modern version of the Long March towards economic viability.

Hard currency is being earned through tourism and a developing export programme of consumer goods ranging from canned lychees to motor bikes.

Foreign investment rules are being relaxed to allow an increasing number of total or partial takeovers whilst cheap labour and tax incentives are persuading more and more overseas companies, particularly European, to move their production facilities to China.

China's shop window to the world is the six-monthly **Trade Fair** held every April and October in Canton, conveniently close to the Special Economic Zones near the border with Hong Kong.

Developed to provide easily controlled areas for trade and production purposes, the Special Economic Zones are rapidly becoming anachronisms as other provincial areas join the business bandwagon.

Nor should one forget the importance of the banking area as the Chinese, born with abacuses in their mouths, learn the rewards of playing the foreign exchange markets. **Hong Kong** has long been considered a conduit into China for money earned in this manner together with other enviable cash flows from clever business investments using Hong Kong as a financial base. The simplistic days of bartering in the shadow of the sea-going, commercial junks is now well in China's past.

Tourism

Since the mid-1970's when China made the first tentative moves to allow Western visitors into her formerly curtained parlour tourism has multiplied into a billion-dollar business.

This has brought tremendous benefits to the Chinese but not without immense teething problems for a country with an in-born disdain for outsiders let alone any modern experience in the handling of visitors en masse.

Any traveller in the Eighties can testify to the chaos that attends the most simple trip.

Root of the trouble is in the transport system. Government planners, with the best will in the world, could not have foreseen the tidal wave of visitors that would ensue when the parlour door was opened, not slowly but with a hefty bang.

Take the national airline for example.

At first **C.A.A.C.** (Civil Aviation Administration of China) coped with the not infrequent delays and over-bookings, even if it meant re-routeing passengers through other cities or on military aircraft.

Lately, helped along by a switch over to computerised systems that are barely better than the archaic hand-written procedures of the past (thanks to inadequate numbers of trained staff and interface problems with other international carriers), C.A.A.C. has a reputation for sloppy service, unannounced schedule alterations, delays of mind-numbing frequency and an apparent indifference in the face of passenger complaints.

The services of C.A.A.C. have since been hived off into a series of provincial services with the international carrier now being known as China Air. It is believed the decentralising of the administration will overcome the problems.

Meanwhile with the overbooking, reconfirmation and ticketing problems it is probably wise to fly in and out of China on one of the many other international carriers servicing the main cities. Within China you have no other choice.

The Railway system is similarly plagued by snafus. Local newspapers report official crackdowns on ticket scalpers which must make the Chinese railways unique in the world. Reports of tourists sleeping in stations awaiting seats previously thought to be confirmed are not uncommon.

Normally one could turn to C.I.T.S. (China International Travel Service) the umbrella service that looked after all the travel plans of foreign visitors. However a new-look administration has made provincial branches of the service autonomous from and competitive to the central Beijing office.

This can create some interesting wrinkles and a guide who knows all the ropes is essential.

> **INFOTIP:** Have your hotel or guide write the name of your destination and your hotel's address in Chinese. This will prove to be a boon if you stray from the main streets and get lost.

In fairness, it is being unreasonable to expect a country the size of China and with a different set of social priorities to make the transition to a totally Western way of thinking. Indeed, it would be an anathema to their culture. So, accept the inevitable with a smile and keep the hardluck stories to amuse your friends and relations when you get home.

However there is a good side to the story too – the hotels. The new initiatives welcoming foreign investment and expertise is most obvious in the range of hotels especially in major cities like Beijing, Shanghai and Canton.

Within a decade the country has gone from a nil balance in the luxury hotel register to a resounding credit. Only Hong Kong would open more new hotels.

With the hotels has come foreign management and whilst stories abound of the difficulties in training Chinese staff the traveller will be pleasantly surprised at the service and the appointments of the major hotels. Sheraton, Regent, Nikko and Shangri-la are just some of the major hotel names represented in the People's Republic.

The increasing freedom within China has meant more opportunities for the independent traveller especially the second-time visitor who wishes to avoid the well-worn routes and sights traversed by the package tourist. Experienced observers suggest that plans should always be made through major travel operators who have the clout when plans foul up. Good contacts are worth more than a fistful of dollars.

Tian'anmen square

Religion

'Without recognising the ordinances of Heaven, it is impossible to be a superior man'.(The Confucian Analects).

Religion has always tended to be a cerebral experience for the Chinese. The philosophical, the metaphysical and the mystical are emphasised at the expense of the emotional.

Religion in China had its foundation in philosophy with a gradual easing into the social fabric unlike the dramatic entry of Christianity into Western society.

Whilst **Confucius** is recognised as the greatest of the Chinese philosophers he was not the first. Chronicles from two hundred years

before the birth of Confucius (551 BC) show that the concepts of Destiny, Good, Evil and Heaven were known and discussed whilst Confucius himself was to go on and expound on these subjects and to formulate what was possibly the first example of the Golden Rule ('do unto others').

Taoism gets the credit for being the first 'organised' religion although it started off as a school of philosophical thought c.350 BC with an emphasis on the rejection of social restraints, the aristocracy and politicians. The stress was on the individual and a mystical union with 'dao', a word which roughly means the 'nature of things'.

By the time of the Han dynasty (206 BC - 220 AD) Taoism had developed an organised format of ceremonies, festival celebrations and monastic orders who, tax-free even in those days, built up such an economic base they proved a threat to the Emperor whose suppression led to the Revolt of the Yellow Turbans, so called after the yellow headgear worn by the religion's followers.

By opening up the Silk Route for trade with the West during the short-lived Qin dynasty (221 BC - 206 BC) **Buddhism** first made its appearance in China from India where it had been already in existence for four hundred years.

Initially Buddhism was looked on as the 'barbarian's' version of Taoism as the Chinese had extreme difficulty in comprehending the subtle nuances of the religion. Later, when the Sanskrit was finally translated into Chinese in the 5th. century AD, the religion expanded and in the later form of Zen Buddhism was to reflect the influence of her new converts.

Buddhism was largely responsible for the development of Chinese literature and the printing process. The Buddhist Diamond Sutra, published in 869 AD, is the oldest known example of printing.

Other religions, major though they might be in the West, were to have a minor effect in the face of such entrenched philosophies. **Manicheism, Judaism** and **Christianity** were all to win converts but not to the extent of Taoism and Buddhism. Surprisingly Islam is said to have more followers in China than in any other country and is catered for to the extent even prisons have separate Islamic kitchens.

Nevertheless religion, for all the part it has played in the cultural, social and even political development of China is officially ignored today. Lip service is paid to freedom of religious thought and worship (guaranteed in the Constitution but with provisos about foreign control). But, in line with Karl Marx's denunciation of it as the 'opium of the people' (sardonically trite in China's case), limited practise is tolerated only by the old and those 'sympathetic' to the communist ideology.

However, in the case of Buddhism, the monasteries and magnificent statues are proudly shown off to visitors without the slightest trace of irony.

Chinese People

As befits such a vast country the population is equally as impressive. Over one billion people now live within the People's Republic. An alarming 80% live in rural villages with the remaining 20% in the cities and the larger provincial towns.

With an illiteracy rate estimated at 25% and only 15% of the land being arable China would hardly fit into the category of the 'lucky country'. However the current Chinese leadership has not shunned the immense task ahead of it. Pragmatically they can see the potentially, powerful base of a large, educated population unlike the Emperors of old to whom the peasantry was merely a source of serfs in peace and cannon fodder in war.

The issue of the 'Minorities' makes the problem of unification and a universal homogeny more complex than it would appear on the surface.

China has approximately 53 minority people as distinct from the **'Han'**, the major racial group who comprise 93% of the population.

Whilst most of the minority groups are situated in integrated pockets throughout the country there are five major groups who are organised into **Autonomous Regions:** Tibet, Inner Mongolia, Xin jiang, Ning xia and Guang xi.

The word 'autonomous' is, of course, relative. The regions have day-to-day autonomy but policy making is still in the hands of Beijing. Cadres from local districts within the regions are sent to the National Minorities' Institute in Beijing for administrative and political training to ensure the Central Committee's wishes and plans are carried out.

'Integration' is the term officialdom likes to use when talking of their policies for the more controversial regions, such as the disputed territory of Tibet. 'Suppression' is the word independent observers use.

Still the government mandarins have been less harsh in recent years and it is possible to visit these regions and for members of the minority groups to travel outside their own borders. Even on the streets of Beijing it is possible to see the distinctive high cheek bones of the Mongolian and the broader, flatter face of the Tibetan. Their national costumes make a colourful contrast to the normally, drab garb of the city dwellers.

The dominant Han race are spread through North and South China roughly speaking along the coastal belt. Those in the south have a slightly different look due to the assimilation of many non-Chinese types. The tourist will readily notice this if travelling, for example, from Shanghai to Beijing.

Similarly, on the crowded streets of Beijing, it is easy to spot those visiting the capital from the rural districts.

The **Han** are considered the true Chinese. In fact, until the founding of the People's Republic it was common to use the symbol for a dog in written descriptions of the minority races. This conformed with the general Chinese attitude to any type of foreigner who was, and still is, considered a 'barbarian'.

The people of China live within twenty two provinces, five autonomous regions, three municipalities and over two thousand counties.

The lifestyle is work and more work. The normal working day is eight hours with a six-day week with strong encouragement to take on self-improvement through study outside working hours. One week's holiday a year is allowed. But this strict regime is being softened with a more enlightened administration now favouring limited private enterprise either full time or part time. Two jobs are not uncommon. Whilst on the other side of the coin employers are being given permission to sack workers who don't pull their weight.

The other face of China

Chinese officials, by the way, don't admit to unemployment.

The urban Chinese either live in traditional, walled, three-sided homes around a small courtyard with relatives or a separate family in each of the three sides or else they are housed in one of the countless apartment blocks that line the streets of Beijing and other cities in seemingly endless rows. Shared washing and toilet facilities and sometimes kitchens are the rule rather than the exception in the courtyard homes. Often public street toilets will service a group of homes.

In apartment blocks a typical flat would consist of two bedrooms, a kitchen with gas cylinder cooking and a combination Chinese-style toilet and shower i.e. a seatless toilet flush with the floor with an overhead shower (one can squat and wash at the same time!)

The homes are gathered together in districts of 56,000 residents under the control of **Neighbourhood Committees.** Under these government-appointed bodies are **Residents' Committees** covering

an average of 550 households each. A group leader for each 'gate' or apartment building is the last link in the chain between the resident and the governing bodies.

It is the responsibility of the committees to ensure the health of the residents and their political education, that news is made known, that the elderly and the young are cared for, that unemployed youths straight from school are gainfully employed and that the wilful are 're-educated'.

Health care is considered important. Efficient clinics are maintained throughout the major residential areas on an average ratio of one clinic to every seven apartment blocks.

Shopping is done in local markets. A family's diet is mainly rice and vegetable with meat in the form of chicken, duck or pork – rarely beef or lamb except in Inner Mongolia where mutton stews are traditional. More imported canned goods are to be seen in shops but prices tend to put them out of the reach of the average, blue-collar family.

Western-style dress is rapidly replacing the infamous 'Mao' suit of a high-buttoned navy or grey tunic with matching, baggy trousers. Southern cities like Shanghai and Canton have long been more cosmopolitan and sophisticated in their clothes. The people of Beijing have been less adventurous no doubt because of the stifling effect of living in proximity to the nation's rulers who are not noted for their sense of fashion. As everywhere it is the young who have made the running in adopting Western dress although Beijing youngsters appear to have settled on the Sixties for their role models and high-heeled, pointy 'winkle picker' boots and skin tight jeans do look incongruous to this Westerner's eyes.

INFOTIP: Although Western dress styles are normal in China, women in shorts and mini-skirts will provoke giggles or frowns. Modesty in dress will be less embarrassing for everyone.

Pleasures are kept simple. Museums, art galleries, zoos, circuses, acrobatic displays and movies are readily and inexpensively available. In the larger cities small restaurants are packed from morning till mid-evening – you are unlikely to find any midnight revellers in China as shift workers need to retire early.

Most seem to take their greatest pleasure in simply cycling through the streets. Even on a winter's evening you'll find the streets crammed with cyclists solemnly pedalling along the gloomy, ill-lit, misty roads. The bike rider is king in China and appear to enjoy immunity from prosecution as they blandly break every known safety regulation. Officials have lost count of the number of bikes owned in China. In Beijing alone it runs into millions.

The other major forms of urban transport are the buses and trains. Beijing has an excellent, fast and cheap underground rail system, whilst above ground ancient buses with bodies hanging out of doorways and windows grind relentlessly through the city and suburbs.

Country trains also suffer from overcrowding. Passengers have a choice of 'hard' class (used by most ordinary Chinese) or the more comfortable 'soft' class (for officials and foreigners). Even when using the same class of travel as foreigners, whether by train or plane, the local Chinese enjoy fares that are considerably cheaper. Which seems entirely fair.

Overall the Chinese are a remarkably resilient race, bouncing back after centuries of subjugation by both local and imported tyrants. The sheer weight of numbers may have something to do with it but many an observer would put it down to the fundamental philosophies that govern their daily life.

Meeting People

The Chinese people have enough historical reasons to dislike and distrust foreigners. The West in particular has had a sorry record of looting, whether in straight out military operations or whether in the name of 'trade'.

Bearing this in mind and considering also the vehement anti-American propaganda instilled into children during the xenophobic days of Chairman Mao it is surprising to find the average Chinese prepared to offer a friendly welcome.

The language itself is a natural barrier to any real dialogue unless the visitor has made an attempt to conquer the complexities of the Chinese tongue.

Still there are always numerous Chinese students who, eager to practise their English skills, will approach you on the street. Mind you, the conversation tends to be one-sided with more questions being asked of you than answers supplied to your questions. And in some smaller towns there is the chance that some interfering, dyed-in-the-wool hardliner or a plain clothes security man will shoo the students away. But it is a chance to bridge the communication gap.

Unfortunately many overseas visitors have an unconscious, patronising attitude to the Chinese. It is too easy to assume a different culture means a lack of intelligence. But you're a guest in a country with a long and proud history of learning already behind it at the time the Europeans were still flopping around in the Dark Ages.

Encounters of the student kind will soon prove how little right we have to be patronising. Quick witted and with inquiring minds they are extremely eager to learn about the West.

These meetings can develop into invitations to private homes and long-term friendships can flow on.

Contact with Chinese whether on a personal level or in an official capacity (business, shopping, travelling) should always take into account the importance of 'face'. The Chinese will not give in to bad temper, threats or demands. Their minds 'close up shop' when confronted with any form of agitation from a foreigner. To back down after making a statement is to lose face and they will quickly retreat into a stubborn attitude that will only be mollified when the foreigner is prepared to compromise. Incidentally when dealing through a third party, such as an interpreter, you will notice a great deal of shouting as though an unearthly verbal brawl has broken out. On the contrary, shouting along with that other charming custom of spitting (still strong despite official attempts to ban it) are two of the less attractive but normal characteristics of the Chinese.

> **INFOTIP:** 'Face' is extremely important to the Chinese. There is no point in prolonging an argument or getting irate when a problem occurs. It is essential to understand that the person you are confronting needs the opportunity to 'save face' otherwise your arguments will be in vain.

One way to establish common ground is when the Chinese let their hair down during one of the major festivals or celebrations.

Chief amongst these is the **National Day** on October 1 remembering the declaration of the People's Republic on that date in 1949. Throughout China there is a holiday and special activities but the focus of the country is on Beijing where a million or so people will gather in the huge Tien 'anmen Square for a giant parade of people and floats glorifying all the major facets of Chinese life: educational, cultural, military and industrial. The leaders of the Politburo review the parade from the balcony of The Gate of Heavenly Peace (Tian'anmen) with its massive portrait of Mao looking down across the Square. Behind this Gate is the Forbidden City.

May Day, another highpoint on the universal Communist calendar is also set aside for special celebrations although not to the extent one would expect. Also of a secular nature are the Chinese **Youth Festival**, the **International Children's festival**, **Woman's Day** and the **National Liberation Army Festival**.

The Chinese still retain festivals from the old culture the main one being the **Spring Festival** which marks the beginning of the **Lunar Year** and despite its title is held in winter at the beginning of February. A four day holiday is allowed at this time and many Chinese take the opportunity to return to their native villages if living away from home (the Chinese generally have no say where they will work – bureaucrats will shunt them around the country often to jobs for which they have the wrong qualifications).

Despite an official policy of atheism the Chinese still practise ancestor worship and the **Feast of the Dead** in April is the time when they pay special attention to the dear departed with burnt offerings of paper money and flowers and by visiting graveyards to tidy up the tombs.

Cakes play an important part in the rituals of the festivals especially the **Autumn Festival** at the end of September when moon cakes are eaten at the time of the full moon. And during the **Dragon Boat Festival** (more fully observed by Chinese communities overseas) triangular cakes are prepared and thrown into the river Mi Lu in memory of the poet Qu Yuan who threw himself into that river in 277 BC.

Naturally Christmas is not observed but New Year's Day is noted with a two day holiday.

Weddings are another good excuse to let off steam and on the morning of the ceremony the local neighbourhood is driven crazy as relatives and friends fire off strings of crackers in a noisy salute to the happy couple. Of course the ceremonies are performed before government officials and not in churches.

INFOTIP: As befits the nation that invented them, the Chinese love fireworks. Any occasion, from a birth to a wedding, is an excuse to let off crackers in the street although rarely will you see fireworks in the sky unless it is a major event.

Language

As indicated above the main stumbling block in communication between East and West is the language

Not only is the fact that 50,000 pictographs or characters make up the complete body of the Chinese written language (in practise a 'mere' 5,000 are used) but, when the language is spoken, phonetic intonations can alter the sense of many words often embarrasingly so for the novice.

There are many dialects throughout China but roughly the country is divided into two sectors. In the North the dialect, and the official one at that, is Beijing often known as **Mandarin.** In the South and overseas the version is **Cantonese.**

Beijing or Mandarin developed from one of two styles of written and spoken Chinese which had their origins in the gradual adoption of a common language around 220 BC.

As the language evolved there were two distinct forms: 'Wenyan' the tongue of the ruling Mandarin class and 'Baihua' that of the literary scholar. Following the eventual downfall of the Imperial dynasties this century wenyan was rejected for its relationship with the oppressive regimes of the past.

The introduction of an alphabetical script in the European style ccame with the work of a 17th. century Jesuit, Matteo Ricci. This was further developed through the centuries until we had a codified Wade-Giles phonetic alphabet which has been replaced in recent years by the Pinyin system. Examples of the change: Peking became Beijing; Mao Tse tung is now Mao Zedong and Chou En-lai becomes Zhou En lai.

Although it has been resisted to date, it will become inevitable that a bastardisation will occur as modern English and American idiomatic words find their way into everyday Chinese use.

As with any country the traveller would do well to take a basic primer on the trip if only to learn the English pronunciations of such common phrases as 'hello', 'thank you', 'how much is it' (asssuming you will be able to understand the reply!), 'a beer please' and 'goodbye'.

When it comes to the written language you will have more problems but it is worth studying the pictographs or characters for such basic essentials as 'male', 'female', 'entry' and 'exit'. Luckily, in the case of toilets, picture symbols are used although as they tend to be of a unisex person you could be in for a surprise, not to mention the surprise of Chinese toilets themselves.

INFOTIP: Unless you intend to spend some time in China it is pointless trying to learn the complicated language. However a few phrases such as 'ni hao' (pron. 'nee how') for 'hello', 'xie xie' (pron. 'shee shee') for 'thank you' and 'gambei' (pron. 'gambay') for 'cheers' are worth memorising, especially the latter.

Literature

The written word charts the history of all countries and its own history says much about the way a nation's growth and its priorities.

Whilst Egypt (1800 BC) and Greece (800 BC) were ahead of China (600 BC) in the field of literature or 'historical records' as they really were, it is arguable if they ever matched China's artistic and practical applications of language.

In style, subject matter and texture the Chinese paralleled the Greeks literary development being rooted in philosophy and history rather than religion. By comparison English literature was very much a latecomer not making an impact till a thousand years later and with a naive roughness when contrasted with the sophistication and poetic depths of the Chinese, and the Greeks for that matter.

Whilst there is evidence that China had a writing system as early as 1400 BC it was not until the 6th. century BC and the birth of Confucius that a literary history started with the Classical Period which lasted until 3rd. century BC. Ironically Confucius, the most revered of all Chinese philosophers, never put pen to paper to record his wisdom. His thoughts were expressed orally and later collected by disciples who produced the books, in particular the Analects on which his fame is founded.

The major work of this period was the Canon, a thirteen book collection which included the Analects, works by other philosophers such as Mencius, various histories and the Classic of Songs the first anthology of Chinese poetry.

Poetry is the binding thread in the history of Chinese literature. One was never looked at askance if one claimed to be a poet. Even Chairman Mao and many of today's political hierarchy are proud of their poetic efforts even if social reconstruction tends to be the theme rather than the romantic, sensuous and philosophic images of the past.

The Tang Dynasty (618 - 907 AD) was considered the richest period for Chinese literature with the emergence of many fine novelists and the refinement of poetic techniques. Strangely enough the next three hundred years under the Song Dynasty were considered by some commentators as less inspiring. At this time there was a strongers emphasis on prose but there was also a return to the earlier oral trad-itions of the storyteller.

The Ming Dynasty (1368 - 1644 AD) corresponding with Europe's Renaissance saw the development of the novel – stories told for their own sake and not necessarily for enlightenment.

The last great period for Chinese literature coincided with the last Imperial dynasty, the Qing, which culminated with the establishment of the Republic in 1912. The latter part of this era, especially the 19th. century, reflected the influence of the encroaching Western powers. Already from the 17th. century major technical, mathematical and astronomical works from Europe had been translated. Later the classics of Sir Walter Scott and Charles Dickens (still a favourite with Chinese readers) became available to the Chinese through the work of Lin Shu.

The Western influence continued into this century and during the 1920's and 1930's, despite the increasing intrusions of Marxist philosophy, writers and poets experimented with the Romantic and Modern schools of literature from Europe.

This was to be the last time they had this intellectual freedom. World War 11 and the founding of the People's Republic of China in 1949 swung the intellectuals into the service of the Party and a plodding dullness replaced imagination. The low point came with the famous 'Hundred Flowers' campaign in 1956 ('let a hundred flowers bloom together, let the hundred schools of thought contend') followed in the next decade by the Cultural Revolution. The philistines under Mao's wife Jiang Qing were let loose and until the rampaging Red Guards were finally brought under control the country's intellectual and artistic life was the subject of constant, vitriolic propaganda and physical attack.

The Cultural Revolution is still in people's memories and even the purging show trial of Madame Mao's infamous Gang of Four has not wiped out the feeling of uneasiness and shame about those dreadful days.

Today the intellectual community is getting back on its feet. To a degree China is turning inwards again to the past. However, with the new stress on education, the cultural atmosphere is encouraging for the slow but sure progress into a new literary era.

The Foreign Language Press, Beijing produce well-printed and inexpensive versions of major, approved works for foreign consumption. These are available at the larger Friendship Stores within China and at specialist bookshops overseas. It is heartening to see more and more Western publishers producing their own anthologies of Chinese short stories and poetry.

Temple of Heaven, Grounds

Theatre

With Chinese literature and art it is possible for the Westerner to appreciate the subtleties and skills of the creative process. Chinese theatre is a different matter.

Even the best will in the world finds it hard to cope with the complex and apparently discordant nature of Chinese drama.

Theatre in China is essentially operatic in nature. The singer is the focal point whilst speech is basically for dramatic continuity. Due to this, the atonal qualities of the music and the harsh (to foreign ears) sound of the Chinese voice, a night at the Chinese opera may be a visual and aural experience but is unlikely to be a mental one.

Theatre does not have the long history of literature or art. It is said to have evolved out of the Court entertainment of the Han dynasty (6th.c.AD) not reaching proper development until the Yuan dynasty seven hundred years later although the Tang emperor Ming Huang established the first drama school, the 'Pear Garden' in 720 AD.

The basis of Chinese theatre therefore was in the antics of the court jugglers, singers, dancers and jesters. To the cynical mind this can still be seen in the highly stylised overacting that takes place on the modern stage in Beijing and other centres.

Straight drama, in the ritual two or three acts as we understand it, is a very new innovation ironically started in Japan in 1907 when a group of Chinese students formed the Spring Willow Society in Tokyo. Their first production was 'La Dame aux Camelias'.

The foreign visitor to Beijing, the home of Chinese theatre, will more likely be taken to a ballet production than to Chinese opera unless a specific request is made. At theatres like the Ah gee 27 you would see, for example, 'The Silk Road Episode' in which an old mythological tale is told with ballet and mime. The costumes are lavish, the music more conventional and the stagecraft professional. Thankfully you are normally spared the heavy revolutionary themes which determined theatrical productions in recent decades.

INFOTIP: Don't be surprised when attending a live theatrical or circus performance to see the cast returning your applause by also clapping. It is customary within China to make this reciprocal gesture. It is also customary for the Chinese audience to leave immediately a performance finishes without applauding.

Art

Of all the Chinese cultures art has been the oldest, the most sophisticated and the most subtle.

As early as 3500 BC quality pottery in white and black was being produced at Lungshan in Shandong Province. The fashioning of superb ceramics has continued in an almost unbroken chain until the middle of this century. Regrettably, other social priorities have meant a drop in the standard of work being produced today. On the other hand the jade carvings being produced today in Beijing and Shanghai are exquisite.

To the unfamiliar eye the paintings of China all look derivative from the one school. Admittedly there was not the profusion of schools of artistic thought as in Europe. But the strength of Chinese art is in the less obvious qualities of a work – subtle suggestion rather than mirror images, which is why calligraphy is also considered an important art form.

Sport and Recreation

Government policy is to encourage sport and the Chinese people, especially the young, are quick to take advantage of any sporting facility available. They show an intense dedication and can be fiercely competitive.

Athletics and gymnastics are basic school and university activities and the more proficient go onto major competitions. Basketball is also popular as a participatory and spectator sport and in international matches China can field teams of surprising height.

But if there is one sport associated with China it is table tennis. Despite the fact the game allegedly originated last century in England and although the alternative name 'Ping Pong' came from the sound of the ball on the bat and not from the Chinese language, there is no doubt the game is looked on as being the speciality of the Chinese. Whatever the reason they took to it with an almost ferocious intensity and have turned a social game into one of skill, tactics and adroit athleticism.

The four 'S's', swimming, soccer, shuttlecock and snooker also occupy the Chinese sports' fan. Snooker has recently gained in popularity and it is common in Beijing to see a communal outdoor table standing amidst dust and rubble with a line of players waiting their turn.

Although classified by some as a sport, Tai Ji Quan or Tai chi, has almost the aura of a religion about it. Anywhere in China, first thing in the morning, you will see young and old going through the intricate and slow routines. Tai chi is attributed with keeping the body supple and the cynical have been known to claim the reason it is so popular is because of the squatting required with the hole-in-the-ground toilets.

The Chinese are also devotees of board games. Xiang Qi, dating from the eighth century AD, and similar to Western chess is one such game you will see played. Also very popular is Tiao Qi which is played with marbles and a board with holes – we know it as Chinese Checkers. Mah jong and a simple form of draughts are also used to pass the time away.

But most of these pastimes are fancied by the old; the young have other recreations, notably television which offers foreign series along with local dramas and educational programmes. Of the latter one success story is the teaching of English which has made cult figures out of the British presenters.

Chinese opera and films attract big crowds as do circuses, zoos and the various museums, palaces and historical monuments like the Forbidden City, the Summer Palace and the Great Wall. And if there is nothing else to do they just mount their bikes and cruise the streets.

The Opera

Cuisine

Undoubtedly Chinese food is the world's most ubiquitous cuisine. From the fast-food, take-away to the up-market restaurant Chinese cuisine is standard fare in countries circling the globe.

In the southern regions and overseas the normal style of food served is **Cantonese** which could be described as an 'all purpose' cuisine. Less oil and fewer spices are used so that there is more of the natural taste of the ingredients. Steaming and stir-frying are a large part of Cantonese cookery which produces such staples as sweet and sour pork, beef in black bean or oyster sauce, steamed fish with ginger and the inevitable fried rice.

For things spicy then the choice should be **Sichuan** and any tourist who has enjoyed one of the regulation banquets in that province can testify to the mouth-numbing, palate-destroying heat of the food.

Beijing food, because of the cooler northern climate, is also spicy, with that city's most renowned dish being Beijing Duck which, at its best, features force-fed young ducks which are cooked by blowing air under the skin and filling the cavities with water which when heated steams from the inside. Beijing Duck restaurants are popular throughout the city but the sheer numbers eating there daily would suggest that some short cuts are taken. In these restaurants all ingredients in the meal come from the duck including jellied ducks feet, boiled eggs, giblets and duck soup.

The Chinese also delight in the exotic and are partial to dishes that would make the average animal lover squirm: bears' paws, snake, fish's stomach and cats and dogs are considered prime eating.

The tourist on the normal package tour will have a set number of banquets scheduled depending on the length of the tour. These can be quite magnificent depending on the chef. In Taiyuan I had the unusual experience of the chef being unhappy with the banquet he had provided and insisting on providing the same twenty-course meal next morning at breakfast, complete with beer, wine and mao tai.

This is a good time to warn you of the insidious **mao tai.** Brewed from sorghum roots, according to one version, it is the devil's own drink. It has the nasty habit of seemingly leaving the mind clear whilst rendering the limbs quite useless.

Chinese beer is excellent and most regions have their own brewery. Wine is starting to improve with European-style vineyards being opened up. Normally, however, the Chinese wine is more like sherry and is served warm in small, special 'tea-pots'. For non-drinkers Chinese spring water is best.

Mythology

Chinese mythology, whilst, in western eyes, is undeniably 'exotic', has a structure not dissimilar to Christianity: there is the same concept of rewards for the good and punishment for the evil, a Paradise, a Hell and a pantheon of gods including a Trinity, a Supreme Being, a loving Queen of Heaven, a roster of subordinate gods equivalent to Christian saints and a full panoply of devils.

But that is where the resemblance ends. The basic belief is of reincarnation for the good, two forms of paradise for the very good and
differing degrees of punishment including obliteration for the evil.

The mythology is endowed with the spirit of the three religions;
Confucianism, Taoism and Buddhism. Plus, a healthy dose of
Bureaucracy. The heavens apparently are organised along efficient,
administrative lines with the gods' subordinates up to their haloes in
paper work: the paradisical days are spent cataloguing, registering
and shuffling paper; even the gods themselves are not immune
having to present a monthly report each. Maybe that's why the
thought of reincarnation is so attractive to the Chinese. A heaven filled
with paperwork would not be that different from hell!

Flea Market

17 Arch Bridge

The Chinese Heaven is structured on different levels with the gods living in separate palaces. With the exception of the trinity of supreme gods the other deities are subject to promotion and demotion although who keeps the faithful on earth informed as to the current, celestial corporate ladder is not explained.

The Supreme Being is the **August Personage of Jade** (Yu-ti), also known as the August Supreme Emperor of Jade (Yu-huang-shang-ti). Often he is referred to as Father Heaven or colloquially as **Mr. Heaven.** The August Personage is said to have created human beings modelling them out of clay (note similarity to Christian belief) and leaving them in the sun to dry. A sudden rain burst melted some figures before they could be brought in out of the wet and, hence, we have the sick and the deformed.

The August Personage of Jade, despite his greatness is actually second person in the supreme triad with the first place being the Heavenly Master of the First Origin with the third place being the Heavenly Master's successor the Heavenly Master of the Dawn of Jade of the Golden Door.

The wife of the August Personage of Jade is the Queen Mother Wang who was first mentioned in ancient, secular legends as being the wife of the Lord King of the East who lived in the Kunlun mountains which form a border between northern Tibet and Sinkiang. The **Kunlun** mountain range, like the Olympus of ancient Greece, is considered the home of the immortals.

One of the main duties of the Queen Mother Wang is to preside over the banquets of immortality for the gods and a select few souls of the departed who, through exceptional goodness during their lifetime on earth, are rewarded with this special honour. At the banquets the guests are fed the peaches of immortality harvested from trees which bear ripe fruit once every three thousand years.

The other deities are divided into the kind of categories that

determine life below: natural phenomena, the countryside, the home, the professions. There is a separate section for the gods of hell. The following is a representative selection.

Sun God and Moon Goddess: surprisingly, when you consider the importance of the Sun in other ancient cultures particularly Egyptian, there is not an overwhelming dedication to this god in Chinese mythology. The Moon goddess fares better with special ceremonies during the full moon of the autumn equinox during which small figures of hares are prominent as the Hare, who makes the drug of immortality, lives in her residence. The Moon Goddess was considered to have been the wife of the legendary archer Yi who shot down nine of the ten suns when they decided to destroy the world through their heat.

The Lady who Sweeps the Sky clear: with her sleeves rolled up and a broom in her hand she clears away the clouds after rain.

My Lord Thunder: the noisiest and one of the ugliest of the gods with the feathers, beak and talons of a bird, clad in a loin cloth and carrying small drums. Apart from his weather chores My Lord Thunder has a punitive role in the heavenly chain and is responsible for the punishment of offenders who have escaped earthly legal action. He is also a family man being considered the husband of **Mother Lightning** and father to several scatty Little Thunders who have a tendency to get into trouble.

The Master of Rain: he sprinkles water from a large pot with a sword and is helped by the **Little Boy of the Clouds** and the **Earl of Wind** who carried the wind in a goatskin bottle although he is said to have been replaced by a tiger-riding woman, **Mrs. Wind.**

The Dragon Kings: they are the in-between kings on a level dividing the gods of thunder, lightning, rain and wind from the supreme deities. The four Dragon Kings rule the four seas and as they also bring rain are prayed to during times of drought. Even in such a·

hard-boiled city as Hong Kong you will find that hotels along the waterfront of Kowloon have big windows looking onto the harbour to enable the dragons living in the surrounding hills a straight passage to the sea. Representations of dragons were often used in the Imperial courts and can still be seen in Beijing's Forbidden City. As well as controlling the seas the Dragon Kings are also considered to increase virtue, favours and generosity.

The Great Emperor of the Eastern Peak: the greatest of the terrestrial gods and one of a group of Gods of the Five Peaks. Reporting direct to the Jade Emperor he is responsible for mankind including births, deaths and the fortunes in between. His abode is Tai Shan a mountain in Shan dong thus endowing the mountain itself with a divinity. Steles there are engraved with the supplications of Emperors down through the ages. The Great Emperor of the Eastern Peak has a vast administration network at his command with registers for the births and deaths of both humans and animals, departments to determine the amount of good fortune one is to have, a department to determine the number of children and an office for reward and retribution. As he also controls the natural phenomena he heads up an administration whose very size must be a civil servant's dream of heaven.

The Emperor Kuan, Kuan-ti: he is the 'ombudsman' of heaven, the god the ordinary people appeal to for intercession in times of personal or communal trouble. His ability to dispel devils and act on behalf of the common man makes him a cult figure. In truth he has a basis in reality, the general Kuan Yu who was murdered in 220 AD by the Emperor of the Wu dynasty after an inter-dynasty war.

The Gods of Walls and Moats: official protector of Chinese cities, towns and villages. This god is the first inquisitor the soul faces after death and his report suggests the path the soul will then follow.

The Gods of the Hearth, Doors, Privy, Place of the House, and Riches: they are common household gods and are responsible for the various components of ordinary family life. One of the more charming customs concerns the God of the Hearth whose representation is a paper drawing rather than a statue. He is honoured with the daily burning of joss sticks and yearly, at the time of his annual journey to the Jade Emperor to make his report on the family, the paper drawing is ceremoniously burnt with a small piece of sugar or similar placed on the mouth of the figure so the god will utter nothing but 'sweet things' when he gives his report. In addition to these family gods there is a range of other gods who look after the various professions including writers, painters, doctors etc. A former dog skinner became the god of butchers; Sung Chiang a 12th. century villain is the god of thieves; a dissolute widow murdered by her father-in-law to stop her lustful ways is now the goddess of prostitutes and an early general who had his toes cut off and used pieces of leather to hide the fact appropriately became the god of cobblers. Farmers have gods of the soil, harvests and ploughing and even the animals get into the act with the God of Cattle-breeding, the King of Oxen, the Transcendent Pig and Lady Horse-head who is in charge of silkworms but got her name after a horse fell in love with her and was skinned for his pains but was still able to carry her off before the August Personage of Jade noticed and to save her changed her into a silkworm.

The After Life

Under Chinese mythology death is not straightforward for the soul is faced with several choices. Depending on the life led the soul can be reincarnated, sent to one of two paradises, condemned to differing levels of hell, completely obliterated or even, if a mistake in the registers has been made, returned to the original body. There is even the chance of becoming one of the deities as all the gods and divine personages had originally been human.

At the hour of death, which time is decided by Shou-hsing the **God of Long Life,** the soul is collected by two attendants and taken to the God of Walls and Moats and kept in his temple for forty-nine days. On the thirty-fifth day he is taken back briefly to his home for a last chance to see his relatives.

In the meantime the **God of Walls and Moats** has prepared a report for the Jade Emperor which has decided whether the soul's time had truly come or whether he had died by accident, murder or suicide for this will establish the fate ahead.

The soul then faces a tribunal of the ten **Yama Kings** whose leader will determine which of the other Yama kings will mete out the appropriate punishment, bearing in mind each of those kings has an individual list by type of the soul's transgressions on earth. In fact the soul will quite likely get punishment from all the kings. These punishments are designed to fit the crime: blasphemers have their tongues torn out, misers are forced to swallow molten gold, others are torn to pieces by wild animals. And they may have to endure the punishment several times e.g. the pieces of the body are put together again and the animals let loose once more.

Once the soul has purged its sins it will go before the tenth Yama king who decides in which form it will be re-born, human or animal. If human the decision will also determine high or low birth. If animal the soul will still retain its human feelings but without the ability to express them due to the Broth of Oblivion which is given by the **Lady Meng** to all souls returning to earth. So if the soul comes back as an animal it will have a human reaction to cruelty and if being slaughtered for food will feel not only the method of slaughter but also the cutting up on the table.

The souls of those who died by accident or through suicide are condemned to hell until they can find someone to replace them by dying in the same manner which is why the Chinese are very superstitious about venturing near the spot where some tragedy has occurred.

Like the River Styx from Greek mythology, the Chinese also include a river, **How Nai-ho,** which has three bridges in the after-life – gold for the gods, silver for the virtuous and an ordinary bridge which cannot be crossed safely for the sinner.

Paradise

Apparently it is the lot of most souls to go through the purging punishments and then be reincarnated on earth.

A lucky few, those who have lived exemplary lives, do get to

paradise. Even here though, it is not a straightforward journey.

The virtuous souls go to **Amitabha Buddha** in the Land of Extreme Felicity in the West.

In this land lakes are covered with lotuses with gold for sand, trees have branches made of precious stones which tinkle in the wind and the air is full of the sound of birds and divine voices.

To ensure complete purity before entering this paradise the soul is met upon death by Buddha himself who places the soul within a lotus flower which will bloom when the soul is ready to ascend into the Land of Extreme Felicity in the West.

Now there is also another paradise. Ruled over by the Lady Queen of the West, the **Queen Mother Wang,** it is situated in the Kunlun mountains on the Tibetan border. These mountains are considered to be at the centre of the world and the sun and moon are believed to revolve around them.

This is the dwelling place of the Immortals and those from earth who through asceticism, healthy practises such as abstaining from cooked food and breath-control, or through a life as a hermit are allowed to join them.

However the person so chosen to live amongst the Immortals has not died, simply transported without his body giving the appearance only of death. There is always a chance he can return to the normal world but if this happens he is entitled to return to the Immortals.,

Apparently life amongst the Immortals is one, big party.

Leader of the fun is the Queen Mother Wang who lives in a nine storey palace made of jade. In the palace gardens grow the **Peach Trees of Immortality,** the fruit of which is eaten by the Immortals.

Life is an endless round of banquets and amusements and should the Immortals ever get bored then their special state allows them to walk upon clouds, fly or go through fire and water without harm.

But overall the common person will take many lifetimes before reaching either of these paradises. In essence it is the Buddhist belief of one's continuing search for Nirvana.

Historical and Cultural Dates

The history and culture of China form such a long, complex pattern that only a multi-volume work could possibly do justice to the subject. The following, therefore, is a surface-skimming project at best and should be read as a basic primer to the events, personalities and cultural developments that contributed in some way to the physical and mental growth of China.

The dates have been grouped together in time periods either by individual dynasties or in groups of dynasties that were noted for specific periods of change.

At regular intervals, where appropriate, there are listed notable events from the world outside China, which occurred during the same period ,to give a comparative framework within which to relate China's growth. These 'foreign' events are enclosed within brackets.

Pre-History

Accepting that early forms of man developed in the African continent it is believed that Homo Erectus moved across to China either via the Middle East and India or even up through Java. This trek took place approx. 700,000 years ago, just prior to the First Ice Age, with remains being found at Lantian in Shanxi province. The first evidence of fire being used for domestic use was found in China. The most notable discovery was that of Peking Man unearthed in Zhoukoudian near Beijing in 1927. Peking Man, from the Middle Pleistocene era, is 450,000 to 500,000 years old.

Neolithic Period. c.7000 - 2200 BC

During this time early man started to consolidate his mastery of the elements. The use of tools became more sophisticated, animals were put to domestic use, the cultivation of crops increased, a primitive interest in art emerged, pagan worship took on a more cohesive shape and interaction between tribes made mankind aware of his social condition.

3500 BC: first chinese city, Lungshan; development of pottery within the Yellow River Valley. (Menes first pharoah of Egypt; earliest examples of Egyptian hieroglyphics; first step pyramid at Saqqara; megalithic tombs along Iberian peninsula and British Isles; Jericho founded; tribes spread through the Americas; invention of wheel and plough.).

Xia Dynasty 2205 - 1766 BC

The first dynasty in Chinese history. Said to have been founded by Yu the Great possibly more myth than man.

It is unlikely there were any actual dominant personalities during this period as it is considered that Yu the Great and the other major heroes Yao and Shun were strictly mythological figures and not flesh and blood emperors.

1800 BC: the use of bronze. (Stonehenge).

Shang and Zhou Dynasties 1766 - 221 BC

These were the most important eras of the ancient world for the

51

fledgling China. The early part of the Shang dynasty coincided with the Bronze Age and as the years progressed the country saw the development of a two-tier social system with a class of nobles who spent their time in leisurely pursuits and war, and a peasantry tied to the land.

These years also covered the 'Spring and Autumn' period (770 - 475 BC) of intense agricultural growth followed by the Warring States (475 - 221 BC) with incessant wars, empire building and general turmoil racking the land. It was also a time when the great philosophers made their presence felt.

c.1700 BC: gradual development of ancestor worship and devotions to a god of the earth; human sacrifices on the death of the wealthy class were common. Emperor acknowledged as 'Son of Heaven'. First settled capital at Anyang. (Glass made in Mesopotamia, 1600; destruction of Minoan Crete, 1450; Egyptian Book of the Dead, 1450; Melanesians reach Fiji, 1300).

650 - 221 BC: Iron technology, 650; Lao tzu founder of Taoism born, 605 (died, 520); Qi, Jin and Chu become three most important centres in China and start inter-city feuding, 600; China's greatest philosopher Confucius born, 551 (died, 479) and founded the 'Hundred Schools of Thought'; landlord class arises as distinct from aristocracy and taxes peasantry into poverty, 500; Warring States period of turmoil and unrest commences and lasts for nearly 200 years, 403. (First Olympic Games, 776; Foundation of Rome, 753; Nebuchadnezzar builds Hanging Gardens, 580; Pythagoras, 530; First books of Old Testament, 430).

Qin Dynasty 221 - 206 BC

Now that the country had consolidated its social structure into a wealthy, ruling aristocracy and oppressive landlord class at the one end of the scale and a downtrodden peasantry at the other end, the time had come for China to move into the next phase. This came about with the power-seeking Prince of Qin who saw personal glory in an overall ruler controlling one vast empire instead of a nation split between several kings.

For seventeen years from 238 when he took control of the state of Qin he waged physical and diplomatic war until he vanquished all competitors and in 221 ascended to the throne as the first Emperor, Qin shi Huang di (Huang di means 'August Sovereign). From his capital, Qin expanded the empire, pushing out the borders and establishing a network of roads and sea routes. He standardised weights, measures, coins and the written language, built the Great Wall and became one of the world's first anti-intellectuals by destroying precious manuscripts and persecuting the followers of Confucius.

These major achievements were made at a tremendous monetary and physical cost to the populace who eventually rose in rebellion and re-established the separate divisions that Qin had broken down. In 206 they dethroned his son who had taken over upon Qin's death in 210. In death Qin also left a legacy in the form of the thousands of life-size terracotta warriors and horses which have been unearthed from his vast burial chambers in the countryside outside Xian. (Ptolemys build temples of Horus, Isis, Edfu, 220; Hannibal's Second Punic War, 218; Archimedes killed, 211).

Han Dynasty and Three Kingdoms Period
206 BC - 316 AD

You could say the Han Dynasty opened with a 'bang' and went out on a whimper. It's founder was Liu Bang the son of a land-owning family and it lasted for four hundred years before the empire disintegrated into a return in 220 AD to Three Kingdoms (Wei in the north, Shu in Sichuan and Wu in the south). If there was a dominating feature in this time it was the emphasis on agriculture with an improvement in irrigation and iron tools and the rise of the landlord class to replace the nobles. During this period a strong merchant class also emerged. By the time of the birth of Christ China's population was 57 million.

The Han dynasty had a reversal from 8 - 22 AD with the installation of a brief Xin dynasty under a former Imperial official, Wang Mang. The Hans returned eventually to have their fate sealed with the Yellow Turbans' revolt of the followers of Taoism. The Three Kingdoms Period lasted ninety six years.

Highlights of this era: the exploration of Central Asia by Zhang Qian, 138; opening of Silk Road linking China with the West, 112; first use of paper, 105 AD; introduction of Buddhism into China, 150; the invasion of China by the Huns, 304 (Julius Caesar invades Britain, 55; birth of Christ; 'Diaspora', the dispersal of the Jews after a rebellion against the Romans, 132 AD; rise of Maya civilisation in Mexico, 300).

Qin Dynasty Stone Warrior

Jin Dynasty, Sixteen States, Southern and Northern Dynasties 265 - 581 AD

There was a brief respite from the divisiveness with a united Western Jin Dynasty from 265 to 313 but a further split came which resulted in the southern area of China falling under the control of five Chinese dynasties, Eastern Jin, Song, Qi, Liang and Chen, whilst the northern regions were split amongst sixteen states mostly ruled by 'barbarians'.

Highlights: envoys visit Funan (Kampuchea) first major Sth.East Asian state, 245; magnetic compass in use in China, 271; Confucianism taken to Japan, publication of 'History of Three Kingdoms', 255; China loses city of Pyongyang to Korean kingdom of Koguryo, 313; building commences of Buddhist cave temples, 350; Turks of Inner Mongolia capture Datong later the Northern Wei capital, 376; Chinese astronomers make first recorded observation of Halley's Comet, 467; silkworms taken to Europe and tea is promoted as healthy substitute for alcohol, 540 (Armenia is first Christian state 303; Samoans colonise Tahiti, 337; Bible translated into Gothic, 350; St. Patrick lands in Ireland, 432; death of Attila the Hun, 453; maize being cultivated in North America, 490; bubonic plague in Europe, 542).

Tang Dynasty Tower

Sui Dynasty 581 - 618 AD

The short-lived Sui dynasty was to set the scene for the advent of the remarkable Tang dynasty that was to follow. The Sui empire came into being under the leadership of Yang Qian, an official of Chinese-Toba descent who fought his way to the top and re-unified the divided country. However he was a big spender building as his capital the largest walled city in the world which, with an area of 7775 ha., dwarfed even Imperial Rome with a mere 1386 ha. Yang Qian also constructed the Grand Canal which linked the Yellow and Yangtze rivers.

The Emperor also had a taste for conquest. He undertook extensive campaigns against the Turks and the Koreans. The Korean wars proved to be the final straw putting such a strain on the economy and resulting in such oppression of the people that it was only a matter of time before they rebelled.

Once again it was a nobleman of Chinese-Toba origins who took over the reins after seeing the effect of Yang Qian's extravagance which had caused the people to rise up in anarchy.

At this stage China's cultural influence was being clearly felt in Japan with the vehicle for this being Buddhism.

The first Buddhist buildings appeared in Japan and even today this cultural 'gift' from China has proved to be more enduring than in the donor country.

It is also interesting to note that, across the vast inland of China, in the Middle East, Muhammed was making his first appearances and the religion of Islam he founded was to have an eventual influence on Chinese culture although not to the extent of the Three Religions — Confucianism, Taoism and Buddhism.

Tang Dynasty 618 - 907 AD

If the West thinks of the Tang Dynasty at all it would be in terms of those wonderful ceramic horses and camels to be seen in the best museums within China and abroad. These are the most obvious manifestations of a period of China's history noted for its cultural achievements, the development of government as a role model for future dynasties and a colonising expansion throughout Central Asia.

Strong-willed emperors followed in the tradition of the Tang dynasty's founder, Li Shi Min, who ruled as Emperor Tai zong from 627 - 649 after first putting his father on the throne, then forcing him to abdicate and executing his own brothers whom he saw as potential rivals.

The period also produced the Empress Wu (690 -705), believed to be the only female to rule China as Empress in her own right rather than as consort or widow.

And as a romantic but tragic counterpoint to a time of cultural encouragement by the Emperor Xuan Zong (713 - 756) is the story that has passed into Chinese legend of his favourite concubine, Yang gui fei, forced to commit suicide by the Emperor's escort who blamed her for his military defeats at the hands of the Turkish born general, An Lu.

The Tang Dynasty saw further contact with the nations in the West as roads, canals and caravan routes were developed. Ideas flowed in as the missionaries of Islam, Zoroastrianism and Nestorian Christianity progressed across the country.

Changan (remembered in the name of Beijing's main boulevard) on the site of present-day Xian was a capital of Imperial splendour with over a million people living within its magnificent walls.

The poets blossomed and the Court saw that music, dance and theatre were given their rightful place. Printing was perfected and the w ld's first printed book was to be produced under the guidance of the Tang emperors.

Highlights: China extends empire and establishes protectorates in Afghanistan and Kashmir, 658; the Golden Age of poetry with Li Po and Tu fu, c700; printing develops, 730; China spreads paper making to the West, 751; first book printed, 853; rebel leader Huang Zhao sacks Canton, 879 (death of Mohammad, 632; completion of Dome of Rock in Jerusalem, 692; Viking raids begin, 793; Charlemagne crowned Emperor of Rome, 800; Norse discover Ireland, 861; Alfred the Great revives learning in England, 891).

907 - 1276 AD

Leading up to the Mongol invasion these three centuries saw China once again divided into warring factions. From 907 - 960 there were the Five Dynasties ruling various parts of northern China whilst the Ten Kingdoms had sway over southern China. A form of stability arose with the advent of the Song Northern Dynasty 960 - 1127 and Song Southern 1127 - 1276.

Under the Song, despite squabbles between the two halves of the country, the merchant class grew stronger and there was a more pronounced emphasis on education and general learning.

Highlights: Vietnam becomes independent of China, 939; the so-called 'barbarian' Khitans establish Liao empire, 947; moveable type printing invented, c1045; Genghis Khan captures Khanbaliq (Beijing), 1215; Marco Polo arrives in China, 1275. (Vikings discover America, c1000; Macbeth murders Duncan, 1040; William the Conqueror kills Harold at Hastings, 1066; Chartres' Cathedral begun, 1154; establishment of first Thai kingdom, 1220).

Yuan Empire 1276 - 1368 AD

Although not a watershed in the history of China, this was still an era of great importance for it marked the first time the country was to be under foreign rule. The infamous Mongols whose campaigns had stretched across to Eastern Europe had now swung towards China. Breaching the Great Wall, under their leader Genghis Khan, they fought their way into the capital which is now Beijing. This was in 1215 established control of the northern half of the country. But it was not until 1276 when the Great Khan's grandson, Kublai Khan, took over the throne as the first Emperor of the Yuan dynasty that the South was brought under the Imperial thumb, with final unification of the whole country in 1279.

China proved to be the base for further Mongol military excursions to Java, Burma and Japan but not with the same success.

The Mongols re-opened the road across Central Asia to the West and with that came a new influx of traders, Franciscan missionaries and Marco Polo whose service in the court of the Khan gave him with the rich material for his renowned book.

Surprisingly, considering the strength and ruthlessness of the early Khans, the Mongol empire in China was to last a relatively short time.

Highlights: second unsuccessful invasion of Japan blamed on the Kamikaze, 'Divine Wind', 1281; first Chinese settlement of Singapore marking a dramatic entry into Sth. East Asia, 1349 (Robert Bruce king of Scotland, 1306; Black death in Europe, 1348; University of Cracow founded, 1364).

Underground Palace Ding Ling

Ming Dynasty 1368 -1644 AD ——————————

Arguably this is the best known of all the Chinese dynasties. It is name synonymous in the West with the finest craftsmanship precious porcelain.

But for the Chinese there were more important things in hand.

The dynasty came into being with the overthrow of the Mong empire with an uprising led by the peasant Zhu Yan zhang (it interesting to note in the long history of China there is no 'dynastic bloodline of rulers as in the West!). It is believed Zhu took the nam Ming, meaning 'bright', from Manichean religious philosophy.

One of the first tasks was to restore the Great Wall, large destroyed during the Mongol invasion.

The dynasty was noted for the greater centralisation of powe culminating with the dictatorial emperor Hong Wu who usurped fc himself more and more control from the government and th bureaucrats establishing a regime of authoritarian oppression of th people and a rabid anti-intellectual stance.

But there were also the great trading expeditions that saw Chines ships sailing into the Indian Ocean and to East Africa. Similarly th adventurous, seafaring Spanish and Portugese had found their wa to the exotic ports of Cathay.

The dynasty fell through the perfidy of the Manchu tartars who had seen the opportunities that lay ahead when called on to help Li Zi Cheng overthrow the last Ming Emperor, Wan Li. It was expected they would return to their homelands once the job was done. Instead they stayed on to fight for their own control of the country which was to lead to the founding of the last of the Chinese dynasties.

Highlights: Chinese traders sail across the Indian Ocean, 1405; Chinese expelled from Vietnam, 1428; Portugese established at Macau, 1557 (Joan of Arc active in France, 1428; Gutenberg prints first book in Europe, 1445; the Renaissance period in full flower with da Vinci, Michelangelo and Botticelli, c1500; the watch invented, 1509; defeat of Spanish Armada, 1588; 'Mayflower' lands in New England, 1620).

Qing Dynasty 1644 - 1911 AD

Not the longest but certainly the most momentous Dynasty in the history of China.

By the time the Emperor Pu Yi had abdicated in 1911 the Chinese people had suffered not only their own round of civil wars, insurrections and Imperial tyranny but also the alien incursions of the 'barbarians' from the West whose plunderings and killings were carried out in the name of 'civilisation'.

This was also the last dynasty. Nearly four thousand years of Chinese history had passed under various Imperial yokes, sometimes as a united country, more often as a warring, divided nation turning in on itself like the imperial dragon of China's mythology.

Equally tragic was the end of a cultural and literary history. Not all the Imperial philistines nor invading factions had ever halted the rich legacy of art, music and literature which continued to evolve in the face of apathy or outright antagonism. However the coming of the Republic was to signal the demise of Chinese culture. Optimistically this is only a hibernation and the thaw in bureaucratic oppression that has come with the Eighties hopefully augurs a resurrection of the traditions that placed China in the vanguard of the arts.

It is amazing that China survived this era intact as a nation, particularly during the latter years.

The Qing Dynasty started inauspiciously with the Manchu overthrow of the Ming Dynasty. The Manchus imposed many of their own cultural values on the Chinese people including the infamous queue or pigtail that was to become a symbol of subjugation.

The Manchus inherited a burgeoning population. At the turn of the 17th. century an estimated 150 million people called China home. By the mid 19th. century this had nearly tripled to 430 million.

Then, as today, this was to be the root cause of the country's political turmoil. Despite a booming industrial and agricultural base the birthrate outstripped the food supply.

China also had to come to terms with the looming menace of predatory neighbours. Under the Tsar, Russia had moved into Siberia in the north, whilst in the south and west there were the perceived threats from the Dutch in Java and the English in India.

Until the end of the 18th. century China was prosperous under the Manchus and relatively free of trouble. The 19th. century arrived and all her worst dreams became reality.

As the country tried to cope with the growing imbalance between people and food the colonising Western powers nailed their ugly colours to the masts of their warships.

England had taken to importing opium from India into China in 1773 to even out the balance of trade. By the 1800's the Emperor was concerned and in 1839 the Imperial Commissioner,Lin Tse-hsu, was dispatched. His edicts and the burning of opium stocks led to the infamous Opium War whose main battles ended with the Nanking Treaty of 1842 which opened up the ports of Canton, Shanghai, Ammoy,Foochow and Ningpo to the British and also ceded Hong Kong to them in two sections: Hong Kong Island and Kowloon in perpetuity; The New Territories on a lease (however in 1984 the British Government of Margaret Thatcher agreed to hand back in 1997 the whole colony and not just the leased Territories).

The Opium Wars in one guise or another continued for another twenty years during which time the Taiping Rebellion occurred and, without the intervention of the Western powers, could have altered the course of Chinese history.

The Taipings were the followers of Hung Hsiu-ch'iian a peasant from south China. Hung's failures over the years to enter the civil service resulted in a nervous breakdown accompanied by 'visions'. Influenced by the teachings of Protestant missionaries Hung came to believe he was the younger brother of Jesus Christ and he had divine mission to rid China of its demons which covered Taoists, Buddhists, Confucianists and the Manchu rulers.

By 1851 Hung was leading a band of followers including a vast number of unemployed. Joined by peasants the campaign initially showed signs of victory with his capturing of Nanking and turning the city into the capital of his Heavenly Kingdom of Great Peace.

The Europeans waiting in the wings saw their opportunity. Taking advantage of the internal turmoil the British and French attacked Peking setting fire to the Summer Palace (1860) and then, sensing the less decisive Manchu government would be easier to control than the rebellious Taipings joining forces with the Establishment to help defeat the rebels.

There was also trouble for China from the East. Japan, in a dispute over Korea, moved into Manchuria whilst inside the capital a former royal courtesan, the Dowager Empress Ci xi, had consolidated power by effectively replacing a weak husband and a weaker son whilst manipulating the Court and the Government and playing the Europeans off against each other. A mistress of intrigue as well as the bed chamber she has a string of executions and murders to her debit.

The secret societies, with which China was riddled, spawned the Boxer Rebellion.

The Yi hetuan or 'Boxers' as they were known by foreigners besieged the Europeans in the Legation Quarter for fifty days in 1900.

Despite the best efforts of Charlton Heston and Ava Gardner it took an expeditionary force from seven Western powers to eventually free them. The Europeans extracted an immense retributive penalty and together with the Japanese grew rich exploiting the country during the chaos that followed.

These events established amongst the Chinese a mood just crying out for revolution.

That mood was sensed by Dr. Sun Yat sen, whose years studying in foreign universities opened his eyes to the opportunities of change.

His chance came with the death of the Empress Ci xi in 1908 and the elevation to the throne of her choice, the two year-old Pu Yi.

The Manchu court officials and government were at loggerheads with each other and the Chinese people. A government move to nationalise the railways was the catalyst for a series of risings culminating in a major rebellion in Wuchang in 1911. General Yuan Shi Kai, an army 'strong man', elected to side with the revolutionaries rather than the Court. Yuan's reward was the presidency of the new Republic of China upon the forced abdication of the infant Emperor.

Highlights of the Qing Dynasty: Treaty of Nerchinsk between China and Russia, 1689; China occupies Outer Mongolia, 1697; occupies Tibet, 1751; Opium War, 1839-42; Hong Kong ceded to British, 1842; Taiping Rebellion, 1850; Treaty of Tientsin opened more ports to foreign powers, 1858; abortive Hundred Days Reform, 1898; Boxer Rebellion, 1900; overthrow of Manchu dynasty by Sun Yat sen, 1911; Declaration of Republic of China, 1912 (Tasman circles Australia, 1645; execution of Charles 1, 1649; Taj Mahal built, 1653; American Declaration of Independence, 1776; French Revolution, 1792; Great Trek by Boers, 1835; Communist Manifesto stated by Marx and Engels, 1848; Commonwealth of Australia declared, 1901; Wright Brothers' flight, 1903).

Republic of China 1911 - 1949 AD

If the ordinary Chinese were expecting their lot to dramatically improve with the fall of the last dynasty they were in for a rude shock. The days of the first Republic were little different to those they had experienced before. In fact, at one stage they almost had a return to Imperial rule.

The army general, Yuan Shi Kai, the first proclaimed President of the Republic when it came into official being on Feb. 1st. 1912, had royal pretensions.

Dissolving the Guomindang political movement set up by Sun Yat sen and then abolishing Parliament he had set himself on an ambitious course to install himself as a new Emperor. Fortuitously he died in 1916 before he could overcome the opposition to his plans.

This plunged the country into further turmoil and for ten years various factions fought for control. The battle was eventually to go in favour of Sun Yat sen who had managed to set up a Nationalist Government in Nanking largely aided by the Soviets.

When Sun died in 1925 control of his government went to Chiang Kai shek who led a right-wing breakaway in conflict with the Communist left-wing faction who, after the proclamation of a central Nationalist Government in 1928, founded a Chinese Soviet Republic in Jiang xi under Mao Ze dong and Zhou En lai.

This proved to be the penultimate split between former colleagues, Mao and Chiang. The Nationalist government then set out to destroy the fledgling Communist party who took to the country with the famous 10,000 kilometre Long March which started in October 1934 and finished midway through 1935 at Yenan in North China.

Chiang Kai shek and Mao Ze dong mended relations in a united front against the Japanese in the Sino-Japanese war that started in 1937, fighting a guerilla war when the Japanese took control of China until defeated at the end of World War 11.

In 1946, with the failure to reach agreement between the central government, the communists and the American advisers, a three-year civil insurrection resulted in the communist troops eventually gaining the firm foothold they had been seeking.

Highlights: Japan occupies Manchuria, 1931; Long March, 1934-5; Sino-Japanese war commences, 1937; Japan capitulates, 1945; Civil War, 1946-49 (World War 1, 1914-18; League of Nations established, 1920; Wall St. crash, 1929; Hitler made Chancellor of Germany, 1933; Spanish Civil War begins, 1936; World War 11 1939-45).

People's Republic of China 1949 -

Chairman Mao Ze Dong proclaimed the People's Republic of China on October 1st., 1949. The 'Great Helmsman' was to chart its progress for over twenty years before advancing age forced him into semi-retirement prior to his death in 1976.

It seems as though destiny was determined to make sure the road was hard and long. Boulders in the way included the Korean War in which China came to the aid of her socialist ally and the introduction of the the Five Year Plans which saw the Great Leap Forward stumble disastrously through over-ambitious plans and a series of devastating floods and droughts.

The Sixties brought two potential catastrophes.

The first was the Sino-Soviet split. In 1960 the two greatest communist powers broke ideological ranks. Kruschev's gestures of friendliness to the United States and the U.S.S.R.'s belief in its supremacy as the socialist leader of the communist bloc irritated the Chinese.

A longtime grudge over the annexation of Siberia and fruitless demands by Beijing for its return added fuel to the fire which soon flamed into a heated dispute. The Soviets cut off all financial and technical aid followed by a series of border incidents in which the Western world watched with amazement and not a little apprehension.

But internally there was more danger in the Cultural Revolution which appeared with no apparent warning in 1966.In the background to the mayhem let loose on the country was Mao and the old guard frightened that the 'purity' of the Revolution was being muddied by revisionist thinking.

For seven years the idealistically, puritanical youth of the Red Guard rampaged through the country brandishing The Little Red Book, the 'Thoughts of Chairman Mao', as a combination bible and banner. It was a frightening, anti-intellectual movement that looted and killed bringing out the worst in the Chinese people who took the opportunity to settle old scores with a ferocity that surprised even the government.

Eventually the death of Mao and a re-alignment of positions and personalities within the politburo swept away the fusty, hard-liners and introduced a new moderate approach to both domestic and international policies.

Architects of these moves were Zhou En lai and the formerly disgraced Deng Xiao ping who ushered in an era of 'rapproachment' with the West and more socially aware policies at home.

The legacy of their work is the China of today, not without its problems because of its population and old-fashioned thinking of an ingrained bureaucracy, but, nevertheless heading down the smoothest road the Chinese people have yet walked.

Highlights: Declaration of People's Republic of China, 1949; Sino-Soviet split, 1960; publication of The Little Red Book, 1964; Cultural Revolution, 1966; joins United Nations, 1971; visit of President Nixon, 1972; death of Mao, 1976; Sino-Vietnam conflict, 1979; agreement with Britain for the return of hong Kong in 1997, 1984 (death of Stalin, 1953; building of Berlin Wall, 1961; Yuri Gagarin, first man in space, 1961, John F. Kennedy assassinated, 1963; U.S. withdraws from Vietnam, 1973; Watergate, 1974).

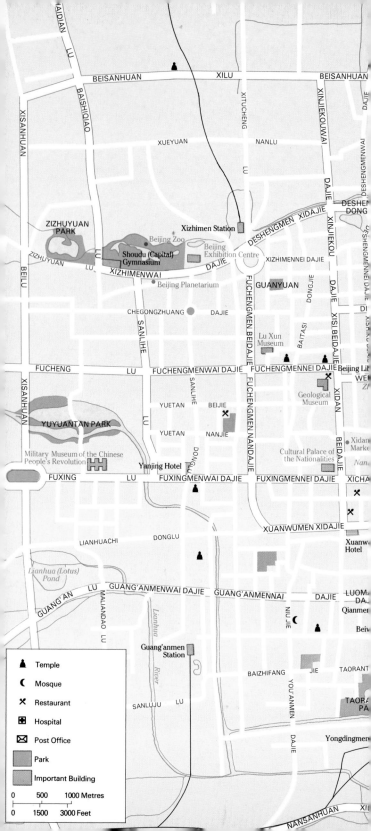

PART II
Sightseeing

BEIJING

HEART OF THE GIANT

'China? There lies a sleeping giant. Let him sleep! For when he wakes he will move the world'.   Napoleon

Whether you liken Beijing to the heart of Napoleon's sleeping giant or to the tale that wags the Chinese dragon, there is no doubt this grey, sprawling confusion of a city is the nerve system of the beast.

The nerve system, of course, is authority and the smell of authority in Beijing is a palpable thing. Just as one can sense the high aroma of power in Washington, here too, through the misty coal smoke and the solid phalanxes of the anonymous millions, there is the same strong awareness that Beijing is the home of the ruling classes of China.

This gives the city a vigor that distinguishes Beijing, for all its dullness, from the the sophistication of it southern sisters, Shanghai and Guangzhou (Canton). The traveller can't help but notice the differences between the three major Chinese cities. Not exactly chalk and cheese. More like the choice between plain and fried rice; the choice between good solid nourishment and a spicy adventure. It's as though being so close to their modern day Gods the people are more content to passivity and conformity.

You can see this in their dress. So conservative, so colourless and so lacking in style.

You notice it in the architecture. Without the dubious benefits of the extensive European 'concessions' that changed the physical face of Shanghai, Beijing remains distinctively prim and unadorned. No Scarlet Woman just the plain, cosmetic-free features of the Ageing Virgin.

In the world of business there is the inevitable form-filling, the waiting, the rituals and the inscrutable blank faces that appear when the problem seems too hard. Even the most modest trading or business transaction from buying an airline ticket to negotiating an export deal becomes an essay in frustration.

The irony is that actual changes are happening.

There are some remarkable, new offices and hotels. People are dropping the drab Mao jackets for coat and tie or, in the case of the young, jeans. On the business front China is actively attracting international investments and her salesmen are familiar sights in the markets of the world.

But this city is so huge, its population so massive, the bureaucracy so cumbersome that you barely notice the progress which gets lost like a weed in a cornfield.

In the light of history this reluctance to change is understandable.

Centuries of continual oppression under various dynasties, regular upheavals and traditional respect for age all contribute to the conservative attitudes of the residents of Beijing.

The latter years have added political stability to the city and although new ideas are taking root there is more a tendency to 'hasten slowly' in Beijing than in Shanghai where Western ways are common place and the distance from the bureaucrats in the north gives greater freedom,

This is not to say that Beijing has remained in the past. The regular traveller can testify to remarkable differences on each visit. In one decade this writer has seen a highly visible opening up to overseas money and the ideas that tag along.

Whether it is the Kentucky Fried Chicken store near Tian'anmen Square, the billboards, the lines of smart limousines on Chang'an Boulevard, the flash uniforms on the doormen at the Kunlun Hotel or the obligatory television set in the meanest home, the progress is obvious, more so than in Shanghai because it has been so long in coming.

Even the treatment of tourists reflects the new opportunism. In 1981 it was the practise for every visitor on one of the packaged tours of China organised by the China International Travel Service (CITS) to be presented with handsome, embroidered table cloths. No journey on the slightly eccentric CAAC planes was complete without an avalanche of small gifts. Alas no more. The cost-conscious accountants with their business degrees from Harvard have seen to that.

As with anywhere else in the world a tourism boom can threaten the charming, if somewhat naive concern for the visitor and switch attention to the contents of his wallet.

Not all is lost. Old Chinese values thankfully linger on nd the tradition of the honored guest is still one of the delightful attributes of visiting this great city.

The language barrier is a hindrance and although shop staff in the downtown area can speak English it is hard to strike up a casual conversation with a passerby, so seeking directions when lost is a major hazard.

Funnily enough, despite the basic grid pattern of Beijing's streets, it is easy to get lost when off the main roads. The crowded roads which have a tendency to wander, the sameness of the buildings and a general lack of highly visible landmarks lead to easy confusion. A good map is essential. If locally printed expect some vagaries.

Modern Beijing is the product of evolving reconstruction during the Ming and Qing dynasties.

As a capital though it can claim a past that goes back to the pre-history of China. The archaeological discovery of Peking Man in Zhoukoudian, in the southwest of Beijing, dates a civilisation in the area back 500,000 years.

As early as the 3rd. century BC, under the Yellow Emperor, Huang Di, there was a settlement in the vicinity known as Zhoulu. His successor Emperor Yao later created a capital called Ji on land a few blocks west of the present Forbidden City.

From then the fortunes of Beijing fluctuated with the tides of war. In 936AD the Khitan captured the city and made it their secondary capital with the name Nanjing (Southern Capital).

But its greatest glory came with the invading Mongols and Kublai Khan who gave it the Han title Dadu (Great Capital), although it was best known by the Mongol name Khanbaliq (City of the Great Kham) which was translated by Marco Polo as Cambaluc. Under Kublai Khan's direction palaces were built amidst landscaped gardens and lakes, moats and walls were constructed and a link installed with the ambitious Grand Canal that stretches 1800 kms. from Beijing to Hangzhou in the south.

During this period the basic pattern was set for the city's

development. Roads were built along intersecting north/south and east/west lines with a uniformity of width: wide streets measuring 24 paces and narrow streets 12 paces.

Further expansion came in the 14th. century with the city's capture by the troops of the Ming dynasty who promptly renamed it **Beiping** (Northern Peace) which a century later, in 1403, became Beijing under Yong Le. Eventually this name was interpreted by Europeans as Peking.

The years of the Ming and Qing dynasties saw the development of Beijing into a gracious metropolis of fine temples, palaces and park-lands. Work was begun on the Imperial Palace or Forbidden City, and extensive new work created the plan for the Summer Palace as we know it today.

This century, with Sun Yat sen establishing his Nationalist Party capital in Nanking, the name reverted to Beiping which held through the tortuous years of World War 11 until the declaration of the People's Republic of China by Chairman Mao on October 1st.,1949 when it resumed the name Beijing.

Since then the city's planners have altered part of the face of the city removing the ceremonial arches, widening the roads and demolishing many old buildings. Luckily they have n't affected its heart.

> **INFOTIP:** Beijing is laid out in an orderly grid system but a couple of odd twists and turns plus the sameness of the crowded streets can be surprisingly confusing, hence the need for a good map. These are readily available at hotels and Friendship Stores.

Chang'an Boulevard

Any city with pretensions to the title 'great' must be able to boast a decent sized boulevard. Paris has its Champs Elysees, New York its Fifth Avenue, Tokyo its Chuo Dori and London has The Mall.

None, however, could be considered as exotic as Chang'an Boulevard in Beijing and in that wonderful paradox that is the East it is both short and long, old and new.

Chang'an Boulevard is only a six-block long stretch running east to west in front of the Forbidden City from Chang Wen Men street in the east to Xi Dan Bei street in the west. Yet it is part of a long road that sweeps thirty eight kilometres through the heart of Beijing from the eastern village of Balizhuang (Eight Li) to Shijingshan (Stone View Hill) on the western outskirts. Hence it is both short and long as befits a city whose boundaries extend eighty kilometres encompassing 16,800 square kilometres making the Beijing over six times the size of Luxembourg.

As to the old and new we need to go back 500 years to the Ming Emperor Yong Le whose reconstruction plans for Beijing included a dirt road in front of the Chengtianmen (Gate That Bears Heaven) on the site where the previous Yuan dynasty's city walls had stood.

In those days it was known as Tianjie (Heaven Street) as it passed the entrance to the Imperial Palace and, for that reason also, it was a banned thoroughfare for the common people. It remained banned

Summer Palace.

until the overthrow of the Qing dynasty in 1912 and the establishment of the Republic. So for the ordinary citizen of Beijing, despite its long history, Chang'an Boulevard, in comparative terms, is really a new street.

Up until the 1950's Chang'an still had its East and West Gates of Eternal Peace and a series of elaborate, three-span memorial archways. These were pulled down and either destroyed or moved to Taoranting Park and a road-widening programme set in motion which also resulted in the loss of many buildings. It is easy enough to dismiss this as the actions of bureaucratic philistines but, in hindsight, the reality of booming population and traffic shows a rare example of forward thinking that has actually paid off.

The visitor should note that the name 'Chang'an' applies only to the six blocks. Up until Chan Men wai the eastern section is known as Jiang Guo Men and after Xi Dan Bei it travels towards the west as Fu Xing Men. As with most streets of any length in Beijing it also undergoes other name changes which can make location-finding a game of chance rather than skill!

As Chang'an Boulevard is what the Americans would call 'the main drag' it is the place to start any exploration of the city. So let's take up our sightseeing there, using Tian'anmen Square as the axis from which we will branch out in the four directions of the compass firstly concentrating on the central section, the real heart of Beijing.

Central Beijing

Tian'anmen Square

The incredible size of Tian'anmen Square never appears smaller with familiarity. Subsequent visits are just as awesome as the first.

To stand at the edge is to look across a plateau of concrete so vast that on a day of pollution you won't see the other end of the 40.5 hectare square.

The grandeur of Tian'anmen is a tribute to the socialist predilection for monumental structures, normally of mind-numbing blandness but in this case quite overwhelming mainly due to the incorporation of the old **Imperial Palace** (Forbidden City) at one end and the impressive South gate at the other.

Originally the square was a third area when built by the Ming Emperors in the 17th. century. The communist government enlarged it to its present size in 1958. Along with the Square it is interesting the care they took with the restoration of the Imperial Palace, like the Russians, showing an appreciation for the artistic splendours of the past if not the regimes themselves.

What is most enjoyable about Tian'anmen Square is its use by the people.

In the past it was the province of the nobles and court officials who would parade under the roofed **'Thousand Bu Corridor'** which stretched for 1.5 kms. down either side of the Imperial Way. The **Imperial Way** itself was reserved for the Emperor on his regular journeys to the Temple of Heaven, in the south of the city, where he would offer sacrifices and prayers at the various seasonal equinoxes and festivals.

Today the square hums with people. The queues waiting to enter the Chairman Mao Mausoleum; farmers and their families up from the country on holidays gaping in wonder at big city life; honeymooners and soldiers posing for the street photographers; elderly grandmothers pushing the old-fashioned, square prams with their charges in those functional, bottomless pants; and, in the early evening, the kite flyers whose traditional pastime adds a pleasantly, nostalgic counterpoint to the throbbing traffic passing by.

Tian'anmen Square is the very core of Beijing and, for that matter, the core of China. As in the old Imperial days it still houses the organs of the central government, the main museums and the gathering places for the people. So it is worth spending some time looking at the life of the square and its immediate surrounds.

Tian'anmen Gate

The visitor will experience that pleasant shock of recognition as soon as the Gate comes into view. It's Mao-bedecked red exterior has been seen in photos all over the world. It is as familiar as the onion domes of the Kremlin.

It was a case of third time lucky with the building of the Gate and the tower. The first wooden structure, built in 1417, was destroyed by fire. Rebuilt in 1465 it again caught fire and when restored in 1651 by the Qing Emperor, Shunzhi, the architects had the foresight to use stone instead of wood. The name was also changed from the original **'Chengtianmen'** (The Gate That Bears heaven to its present 'Tian'anmen' (Gate of Heavenly Peace).

You will notice five archways inset into the main building which were entrances into the Forbidden City, with the wider central door reserved for the Emperor. Five marble bridges over the optimistically named **Golden Water Spring** (Jinshui) link the square with the building. Also of interest are two, 10 metre high marble pillars each topped with a marble **'lion dog'** gazing up to the skies. Their purpose was to catch the 'jade dew' which the Emperor drank to give him longer life – considering the state of the normal water supply it no doubt worked! The lion dog (bou) was also responsible for keeping the monarch on the straight and narrow and, according to legend, would warn him when he had neglected his official duties for too long in the pursuit of pleasure. Today's equivalent being the tabloid newspaper.

The structure of the Gate is tremendously impressive. Standing at its foot you gaze up over thirty metres to the yellow-tiled roof with its decorative dragons, symbolic guardians of the residents within. About two-thirds of the way up, where the pagoda-shaped building begins, are the balconies where the communist hierarchy review the May Day and October 1 parades. Recently this has been opened up to the public, for an extra entrance fee, of course, but the view justifies the minor expense.

Tian'anmen Square

大清國慈禧皇太后

From these balconies Imperial proclamations were let down in a special basket fashioned from gold in the shape of a phoenix with the proclamation being placed in the mouth of the bird, hence the Chinese expression 'from the mouth of the **Golden Phoenix**' when referring to government decrees. Ironically the last time it was used was to hand down the abdication decree for the last emperor, Pu Yi.

It's probably a good idea to climb up to the **Gate Tower** balcony to get your bearings and enjoy the view before setting off across the Square.

Back at ground level don't try to cross Chang'an Boulevard unless you have a death wish or it is 2 am. The traffic is non-stop, tightly packed across the full eight lanes and there are no nearby traffic lights. However at either end of the Square there are underpasses for pedestrians. Use these.

Having negotiated Chang'an let's commence our walking tour around this greatest of the world's squares. A leisurely amble would take an hour. With visits to the various buildings you should allow the best part of the day including a break for lunch in one of the famed Peking Duck restaurants in the shopping district below the South Gate.

Great Hall of the People

With lines of pencil pines and cypresses softening the immense bulk, the Great Hall of the People, or **National People's Congress,** stretches for a third of a kilometre along the western side of Tian'anmen Square.

Looked at square on, you will see a deep u-shaped building with the central section recessed back from the north and south sections which present a facade of collonaded porticos.

If Congress is not sitting you can go inside and be suitably impressed by the halls, auditoriums and various chambers and offices that fill up the 171,000 square metres of space.

The Central Hall, inside the massive bronze doors, is notable for the five, crystal chandeliers designed in traditional Chinese lantern style. The light reflects off the pink marble floor and the white marble pillars.

The main auditorium can seat nearly 10,000 delegates who are housed in a chamber the size of tennis stadium, with the ceiling centrepiece being an enormous red star in a large cluster of lights.

Nearby is the banquet room where Richard Nixon was entertained to a small, intimate gathering of some 5000 for a full sit-down banquet on his history-making visit in 1972.

Amazingly the whole building was constructed in just ten months during 1958/59. Regular building workers and soldiers were supplemented with vast numbers of 'voluntary' helpers including students and professional men. One advantage of a large population is the endless supply of labour as our next stop also proves.

Chairman Mao Mausoleum

In a country where religion is barely tolerated and where there is an official policy of atheism, it strikes the observer that Maoism no doubt serves as a substitute form of worship.

To see the endless queues waiting in reverential silence for hours, just to visit the tomb of a man whose reputation the modern day leaders are quietly diminishing, is to watch a religious ritual. The only things missing are the robes, the incense and the public prayers.

Everything else is there: the strictly enforced, solemn, silence; the cathedral-like interior of the tomb; the thoughtful obeisance of the faithful.

And let's not forget the outpouring of grief at Mao's death in 1976 was followed by a remarkable demonstration of devotion when hundreds of thousands came voluntarily from all over China to work on the construction of this elaborate, contemporary Taj Mahal.

Like the Great Hall of the People the Mausoleum was built in just ten months.

33 metres high and covering an area of 20,000 square metres the building contains two floors of which only the ground floor is open to the public. The exterior has, as a focal point, twelve octagonal pillars of Fujian granite on each side, surrounded by white marble balustrades on a base of red Sichuan granite. The public area comprises a North Hall, a South Hall and a Hall of Mourning.

Western visitors are usually taken to the head of the queue. No photographs. No bags. No talking.

The first thing you see upon entering is a gigantic, white marble statue of Chairman Mao sitting in an armchair with a 24 metre tapestry depicting rural scenes as a backdrop.

From here the slow column moves through the tall, timber doors, past the guards in dress uniform, into the inner Hall of Mourning. Here a crystal casket containing the embalmed body of Mao lies on a black bier sporting the symbols of the People's Republic of China, the People's Liberation Army and the Chinese Communist Party.

The body, dressed in a grey Mao suit, looks distinctly unwell.

As the line is continually moving there is no time to stop and reflect, so before you know what has happened you are being ushered through the South Hall, past a sample of his poetry in his own calligraphy, and shooed outside. All done with a minimum of fuss.

Qianmen

Behind Mao's Mausoleum, at the southern end of Tian'anmen Square and acting as a sentinel between the commercial district and the Square is Qianmen, 'Front Gate'.

Qianmen is a high, double gate-tower erected by the Emperor Yong Le in 1419. The towers on top were destroyed by fire in 1900 during the Boxer Rebellion and again in the 1930's.

This was the final portal in the restricted central area through which the Emperor passed on his way to pray at the Temple of Heaven several blocks to the south. Nowadays it is used by anyone who cares to pass through the red brick tunnel of the tower. More often than not it is used as a thoroughfare by the thousands flocking from the buses that have transported them into Beijing to pay their respects to Chairman Mao.

Together with Tian'anmen, Qianmen forms the last of the remaining four major gates into the city. The other two, Chan Men and Jiang Guo are remembered only in the names they have given to the respective western and eastern sections of Beijing's main avenue.

Monument to the People's Republic

It is claimed this is the first and largest memorial built in China in modern times i.e. since the declaration of the People's Republic of China. Whilst certainly large enough it pales into insignificance compared to the enormous structures erected in neighbouring North Korea.

A 38 metre high obelisk in the central plaza of Tiena'anmen Square, the Monument to the People's Republic took six years to build, unlike the nearby Mao Mausoleum and the Great Hall of the People which were erected in a record ten months apiece. It was unveiled by Mao and Zhou En lai on May 1, 1958.

17,000 separate pieces of marble and granite weighing over 10,000 metric tons were used in the construction of the obelisk whose base is a double-level dais reached by two flights of steps and surrounded by marble balustrades.

White marble from Fangshan on the outskirts of Beijing was used for the various bas-reliefs whilst mauve granite from Fushan was used for the central column.

As well as carvings of peonies, lotuses and chrysanthemums to symbolise 'nobility, purity and chastity', there are two major inscriptions. The first in Mao's calligraphy proclaims 'Eternal Glory to the People's Heroes' with the word 'eternal' striking a strange chord in a country avowedly atheistic.

The other, longer inscription is also by Mao but is a rare example of Zhou En lai's calligraphy and reads:

'Eternal glory to the people's heroes who laid down their lives in the people's war of liberation and the people's revolution in the past three years. Eternal glory to the people's heroes who laid down their lives in the people's war of liberation and the people's revolution in the past thirty years. Eternal glory to the people's heroes who from 1840 laid down their lives in the many struggles against internal and external enemies, for national independence and the freedom and well-being of the people'.

Whilst it reads more like a political tract than a eulogy it has to be understood in the light of the events since the Opium Wars and the intervention of Western powers in the affairs of China.

A pictorial explanation for the inscription is given in the series of bas-reliefs decorating the column. In chronological order they start on the eastern face with the destruction of crates of opium in 1842 by the Imperial mandarin Lin Zi xu followed by the start of the Taiping Rebellion in Guang xi in 1851. Moving round to the south side you will see a representation of the rising against the Manchu in 1911 under Wu chang and two major demonstrations: one held in Tian'anmen Square in 1919 (against the Treaty of Versailles which gave the former German possessions to Japan instead of back to China) and the other in Shanghai as a protest against the Japanese and the English in 1925. The 1927 Nan chang military uprising is portrayed on the western face along with scenes from the protracted guerilla war against the Japanese from 1937-1945. The final frieze on the north side is of the crossing of the Yangtze river by the Communist troops in their successful takeover of the country in 1949.

The monument itself was used as a rallying point in 1976 for a major demonstration labelled the Tian'anmen Incident. It was a two-fold gathering: to mourn the passing of Zhou En lai and to protest at the activities of the Gang of Four.

The **Tian'anmen Incident** was important in the political history of modern China for it marked the passing of the era of Chairman Mao who was to die six months after the event.

The Incident started in late March 1976 during the Qing Ming Festival when the Chinese gather to honour the deaths of their loved ones and those of notable figures, in this case Zhou en lai, who was perceived as being the bastion of reason and moderation after the fanaticism and turmoil of the Cultural Revolution which had been encouraged by the extreme left of the party and the ageing Chairman Mao. So, it was also a public rebuff to Mao who had become increasingly remote from the people.

As was the custom wreaths were laid at the Monument. On April 5th., under orders from the leftists, troops removed the wreaths and arrested any who tried to stop them.

The 'bush telegraph' was activated and within hours tens of thousands had congregated in the square to be met by an armed Workers' Militia. The people lost as did Deng Xiaoping who was blamed for the demonstration. Deng had only just been re-instated

by Zhou En lai after falling from grace during the Cultural Revolution. Ironically it was a case of 'third time lucky' for Deng as he returned to power in 1977 and was to become the powerful force who led the Chinese from out of the doctrinaire closet and into the heady air of capitalism in the 1980's.

The **'Gang of Four'** were less fortunate.

The quartet, under the leadership of Mao's ambitious widow, Jiang Qing lost their ideological war. Jiang along with three other Maoists, Yao Wenyuan, Zhang Chunqiao and Wang Hongwen were put on trial in 1980 accused with an assortment of political crimes including the plane crash death of party stalwart Liu Shao qi.

In a lesson learned from Stalinist Russia the Chinese staged the show trial to end all show trials. Full use was made of the fledgling television service with tapes of the trial actually being supplied to foreign news services. Death sentences were demanded and handed down but later commuted.

To what extent the Chinese use the Monument to remember these events is difficult to estimate. But what is obvious is the continual crush of people around the memorial all exhibiting a more cheerful attitude than one would expect to see at a similar war memorial in the West.

It is also interesting to observe that the centre of Tian'anmen Square with its wide open spaces, the Mausoleum and the Monument to the People's Republic has much more attraction for the average Chinese than the political headquarters on the western side or the history museums on the eastern side. It serves the same function as squares around the world: a place to meet friends, to take the children and to rally on important occasions.

INFOTIP: Singing birds provide companionship for the older Chinese who tend them carefully and proudly parade the small birds in their cages at Sunday morning gatherings in the local park. The younger Chinese seem less interested in this ancient custom.

MUSEUMS

Museums of Chinese History and the Chinese Revolution

These twin museums housed in the one, sectionalised building stand on the eastern side of Tian'anmen Square in symmetrical proportion to the Great Hall of the People on the other side of the Square.

Separated by a central entrance hall the museums occupy two wings. It is carefully pointed out, no doubt 'tongue in cheek', the **Revolutionary museum** is in the left wing. But that depends which way you are facing.

The museums were built in 1959 as part of a government project for ten monumental buildings in Beijing. Consisting of four storeys they stretch for 300m. along the Square.

As you enter the Central Hall you will pass two pillar-shaped torches which symbolise one of Mao's many aphorisms: **'A single spark can start a prairie fire'.**

Inside the Central Hall you will find the busts of Marx, Engels, Lenin and Stalin though don't be surprised to discover Stalin missing as China with the bulk of the Communist bloc has become disenchanted with the tyrant.

Before you proceed into the museums get a copy of the English language catalogue of the exhibits. It is only a few yuan and without it you will only be guessing as to the various displays for the signs are all in Chinese. This is common throughout China and rather surprising considering the majority of tourists speak no Chinese.

There's also a bit of a 'con' with the exhibits, especially in the **History Museum.** Many are not what they purport to be, instead are very good reproductions such as the supposed bones of the Peking Man. Similarly much use is made of photos rather than the actual specimens.

But amongst the 30,000 or so pieces you will find some genuine goodies including a wonderful blue-glazed lamp from the era of the Six Dynasties of the 3rd. to 6th. centuries AD.

The History Museum is basically in five eras: Primitive, Slave, Feudal, Capitalist and Socialist.

Similarly the Revolutionary Museum covers five periods too: Founding of the Chinese Communist Party (1919-1921), First Civil War (1927-1937), Second Civil War (1927-1937), Fight Against Japan (1937-1945) and Third Civil War (1945-1949).

This neat symmetry also applies to the internal architecture as each museum has its introductory hall and seventeen exhibition halls. As there are over two kilometres of hallways allow yourself plenty of time for your tour.

Having finished your sightseeing through the museums you will now be back at Chang'an Boulevard and the Tian'anmen Gate. Behind this gate is the entrance to a wonderland that not even Alice could have dreamed of. It is a world that no Westerner will ever fully understand and that few Chinese ever had the privilege of entering. It is a world that is part history, part legend. A world of fabulous wealth, of political intrigue, of unbridled power and unthinking cruelty. And yet, that world is now but a shell – a facade, a movie set that was not from a scriptwriter's imagination but created from the reality of old Imperial China.

The Forbidden City

Officially it is **The Imperial Palace Museum.** In truth that is correct for what we call the Forbidden City is only the central section of that part of Beijing which became a city in itself known as 'Huang Cheng' or Old Imperial City. This was reserved for select members of the court and government to the exclusion of the rest of the population who lived in the greater part of Beijing outside the walls of this enclave. To enter through these walls without permission meant instant death. The public were finally admitted upon the overthrow of the Qing dynasty and the proclamation of the Republic of China in 1912, although the last Emperor, Pu Yi, and his family were allowed to retain private apartments there until 1924.

Within this city-within-a-city was a further walled section know as the 'Zijin cheng', or Purple Forbidden City, where the Emperor, his relatives and the inner circle of the **Imperial Court** lived and left only for religious observances at the Temple of Heaven or in time or war. The colour purple was the symbol of the North Star and the royal residence thus was regarded as the cosmic centre of China.

It is this latter portion, the Zijin Cheng, that is the beehive to which the swarms of tourists flock each day (except Monday when it is closed).

There had been a palace of some form or other in this general area since the days of the Yuan dynasty (1279-1368) but the plan that inspired the current palace was the work of the Ming Emperor Yong Le who supervised the construction over a fourteen year period from 1406-1420

100,000 artisans and from 200,000 to 1,000,000 workers were used to fashion the splendid palaces, halls and official quarters from stone quarried near Beijing and with wood axed from the forests of Yunnan and Sichuan.

One theory is the basic design is that of a tent with many of the buildings using pillars rather than walls to support the roofs.

Because the Forbidden City has been rebuilt more times than an ageing actress, much of what you see today is of relatively modern construction, dating from the 18th. century.

Thanks to the wooden nature of the complex the palace buildings were particularly susceptible to fire. Numerous blazes started by lightning, faulty lanterns or the odd pyromaniac in the royal family meant the Forbidden City was in an almost constant state of rebuilding.

The eunuchs of the court, who wielded more power than their 'diminished' status might indicate, would often arrange for fires to be lit so they could make a financial killing with kickbacks on the repair bills.

In 1664 the Manchus razed it to the ground.

Equally destructive were the lootings this century by the Japanese and Chiang Kai shek's Kuomintang who spirited out of the country thousands of rare manuscripts and objets' d'art.

Even in recent years there have been changes which will disappoint the visitor making a return trip: most of the treasures within the various Halls have been removed and the Halls closed. Whereas in past years you could wander through the various Halls and delight in the treasures they contained, nowadays you can only peer through the doorway into a gloomy chamber dispiriting in its emptiness. The pressure of tourists (up to 20,000 a day in peak periods) is the legitimate excuse for closing the Halls. No excuse is offered for removing the artifacts.

The Forbidden City occupies 73 hectares within the ten-metre high walls. There are around 9,000 rooms: the more enthusiastic and imaginative guides like to say there are 9,999 rooms, just one short of the divine number,10,000. Still, as you cannot enter all the rooms anyway, and it would be doubtful if you wanted to, the correct number is purely academic.

Surrounding the grounds, outside the walls, is a fifty two metre wide moat which served not only as a defence but as a water supply for the aforementioned fires as the local Beijing fire units were considered too lowly to be allowed inside the city.

Entrance was gained through four gates, north, south, east and west. Today's visitor uses the north or the south.

Gate of Supreme Harmony

Wumen Gate

This is the major entry point. At the southern end, separated from Chang'an Boulevard by the Tien'anmen Gate, it is also known as the Meridian Gate or Five Phoenix Gate.

As you come out of the tunnel-like entrance of the Tian'anmen Gate you will face your first obstacle. The huge square in front of the Wumen Gate will be filled with tourist coaches, taxi touts and bicycles, all of which need to be negotiated before coming to the Gate itself. Incidentally, if you wish to make a visit to the balcony of Tian'anmen Gate you branch off to the right before you enter the square.

At the Wumen Gate you will see three entrances through the lower wall. In the Imperial days the central, wider entrance was solely for the use of the Emperor who would leave through this gate to visit the **Temple of Heaven** or the **Altar of Earth** to the sound of bells and gongs; if he was visiting the **Imperial Ancestral Temple** drums would be beaten instead.

The western entrance, the **Xiahuamen,** was for the army whilst the civilians would use the eastern gate, the Donghuamen which is used today as the main entrance for tourists who will need to run a gauntlet of hawkers offering for hire cassette guides to the Forbidden City — these are not a bad idea if you are making an independent visit without a Chinese guide.

The Wumen Gate was originally built in 1420 and substantially restored in 1647 and 1801.

It played an important role in the administration of external affairs by the emperor. Here he would review his armies, deal out punishment to criminals and announce annually the calendar for the forthcoming year. As the palace was considered the cosmic centre of China so the emperor was considered the only one able to determine the future of the coming year.

He would also grant imperial audiences which were often held before sunrise.

Surmounting the gate is a long, double-roofed tower whose weathered tiles still show the yellow glazing which is the prerogative of imperial households.

Branching off on either side of the gates are the auxiliary buildings of the court and the administration now housing some poorly lit but interesting exhibitions of old pottery, ancient coins and relics.

In many ways the Wumen Gate is one of the most exciting for the visitor because as you come out of the darkened interior onto the balcony overlooking the forecourt to the Gate of Supreme Harmony, you find yourself confronted with the first of the many splendours that await you within the Forbidden City.

Gate of Supreme Harmony

Tai He men, the Gate of Supreme Harmony, rebuilt in 1890 and guarded by two stylised lions representing the power of the empire, is the true start of the Forbidden City complex which extends beyond here in three central sections readily accessible to visitors although the side chambers are generally closed; some, housing temporary or permanent exhibitions, will be open depending on any restoration work, the time of year, the position of the moon, the whim of museum officials — that kind of thing.

The first section contains, on one large raised level, the three main halls; the second section has the two major palaces together with another hall; the third section comprises the **Imperial Gardens** and pavilions.

The Gate of Supreme Harmony gives a splendid view of the 30,000 square metres of courtyard which separates the Gate from the Hall of Supreme Harmony. The courtyard could hold up to 90,000 people and, with the required banging of the head on the ground nine times when the Emperor approached, the noise must have rumbled like thunder throughout Beijing.

Italian film director Bernardo Bertolucci, the first major Western director to be allowed to film within the Forbidden City, captured the grandeur of those mass audiences in his spectacular film 'The Last Emperor' which, although criticised by the Chinese for many errors in fact and detail e.g. costumes, still gives the modern audience the rare chance to see the true glory of those times.

On either side of the courtyard, which now looks rather tatty with unkempt weeds growing up between the flagstones, are two minor halls: on the eastern side the Hall of Manifest Benevolence; on the western side the Hall of Enhanced Righteousness.

In the Imperial era the courtyard was also surrounded by various galleries containing clothes and ornaments for the palace officials, repositories of precious gems and booty captured in battle.

Hall of Supreme Harmony

This is the largest and the most impressive of all the palace buildings, being the biggest wooden palace in China. It is the first of the three major halls we are to visit.

Originally built in 1420 the Hall of Supreme Harmony (Tai he dian) was rebuilt in 1697 to the noble proportions we see today. It is 35 metres high and occupies 2,400 square metres. Supporting the roof are twenty four columns, each made from a single piece of wood 13.8 metres long, the central six columns being carved with gilded dragons.

Entrance to the Hall of Supreme Harmony is three flights of marble stairs onto the surrounding terrace. As with the other halls and palaces you will see, in the middle of these steps, an ornately carved ramp of marble. This ramp was for the exclusive use of the Emperor whose sedan chair would be carried up or down the ramps and not the steps. The ramps are roped off so that any would-be modern emperors don't damage the weather stained carvings.

On the terrace is a large, bronze turtle, a symbol of longevity and stability. On state occasions incense would be placed in the turtle's interior and the smoke would issue out of his mouth; this was in addition to the eighteen bronze incense burners going like the clappers inside the Hall.

Also on the terrace are the musical stones and golden bells to be played for major events so that building was also known as the **Hall of Golden Bells** and sometimes as the **Hall of the Golden Throne** after the magnificent royal chair which, raised on a dais, dominated

Hall of Dispelling Clouds

the luxurious interior. Regrettably you won't get to see that interior as the Hall has been closed to all visitors and the treasures removed so most you can hope for is to peer through roped doorway at a rather gloomy, empty space and try and imagine what it must have been like with the rich tapestries, the ornate chandeliers, the gilded furniture, the cloisonne cranes and the eighteen incense burners representing the eighteen provinces of China.

The Hall of Supreme Harmony was the centre for the more important festivities: the Emperor's birthday, New Year, winter solstice and the announcing of the successful candidates in the Imperial Exams.

The pomp and splendour matched anything the Western nations could offer with the added touch of Oriental exotica. As gongs and bells sounded, the imperial musicians played appropriate melodies whilst the fragrant incenses wafted their smoke up through the thousands of banners and flags that festooned the palaces and the streets outside the walls.

In gorgeous silk costumes covered with the extravagant embroideries and wearing the most splendid head-dress the Emperor would be carried in his chair, accompanied by the richly robed officials and eunuchs, past the throngs 'kow-towing' in the courtyards, through the various palaces and halls (often stopping for a ritual rest) before reaching his throne in the Hall of Supreme Harmony where the **'Son of Heaven'** would perform the required duties. Often he would rest here before continuing on the longer journey outside the Forbidden City to the Temple of Heaven.

The original emperors who built this hall knew the importance of lavish furnishings, if only for the ego.

Hall of Complete Harmony _____

This is the smaller of these three halls. The Hall of Complete Harmony (Zhong he dian) is also known as the Hall of Middle Harmony and the Hall of Perfect Harmony. Like so many of the buildings it was constructed by Yong Le in 1420 with restoration in 1627 and 1764.

As part of the rituals that governed the daily life of the emperors this hall was used as a rest stop prior to leaving for the Hall of Supreme Harmony. One assumes these rest breaks were ritualistic rather than due to the royal personage's inability to make the distance, as the journey was a mere hundred metres or so. Of course the sedan-chair bearers would have been glad of the breather as it was their duty to carry the emperor everywhere within the palace — he never walked. It wasn't really until the last emperor, Pu yi, that this tradition was broken and then with extreme gusto as Pu yi took to riding a bicycle through the palace grounds.

Anyway the Hall of Complete Harmony served other important purposes as well. Within this small, square edifice the emperor would rehearse for the various civil and religious ceremonies, review the long rota of sacrificial prayers he would be required to make, greet foreigners, deliver addresses to the many royal offspring (with several wives and hundreds of concubines he could easily produce a school load of progeny), receive tributes and congratulatory documents from local officials and even examine the seeds required for the annual plantings.

Unfortunately, as pointed out earlier, there is little evidence of these activities for the modern visitor. Imagination is your best guide.

Hall of Preserving Harmony _____

The Bao he dian is the final hall in this section of the Imperial Palace and like the previous Hall of Complete Harmony it was built in 1420 and went through rebuilding and restoration at the same times too.

The Hall of Preserving Harmony (n.b.: not all these wonderful titles bore a direct relation to the activities within) was a major centre for important feasts like New Year's Eve and the 15th. Day of the Lunar Month.

For the 'yuppies' of those days it was the most important building of all. Here the emperor would conduct the **Imperial Exams** which, for the successful, meant instant success, wealth and status. The students, who had made it through the preliminary sorting-out, would gather in front of the throne and write articles to the questions posed by the emperor.

Apparently, as most of the questions would relate to how the emperor could keep and consolidate his power, the more shrewd amongst the sycophantics would pass and receive the coveted title of 'Jinshi' (scholar).

Outside the Hall is a 250 ton marble block which is carved with dragons and clouds and serves as a ramp for the royal progress from the ceremonies. Sixteen metres long it is often referred to as the 'Dragon Pavement'. It was quarried in one piece from marble pits south-west of Beijing and transported to the Forbidden City in a most ingenious manner. It was done during the middle of winter. Workers would dig wells every half-a-kilometre along the way, draw out the

water and spread it on the roads where it would turn to ice. The massive marble slab was then loaded onto a flat-bottomed boat which was slid along the ice. Interestingly enough this method of transportation has been put forward as an explanation for the carrying of the monolithic slabs that form Stonehenge in England.

Inner chambers in the Hall of Preserving Harmony were used for the storage of gifts from foreign powers which were usually treated with disdain and in fact, rarely opened. Up until recent times these gifts, still in their original wrappings could be viewed along with the fine collection of funerary objects and 5,000 year-old embroideries.

As mentioned earlier the emperors loved the lavish trappings of power, if only for self adornment.

But they also understood that the complicated rituals, the luxury of the surroundings, the mystique behind the closed walls and the autocratic rule were all part of the process of keeping the common people subservient. Needless to say they shamelessly traded on the superstitions of Chinese mythology, of which they claimed to be part, as the 'Sons of Heaven'. Ironically, the continued rule of the emperors was not dynastic. Unlike Europe, where blood ties determined accession to the throne (Great Britain being the most notable example), in China it was the case of the strongest and most scheming — even peasants made it to the thrones of the Forbidden City.

And so we have the reasons behind the structure of the Imperial Palace with the various halls and palaces each having a defined roll starting with the above 'introductory' chambers and now leading up to the inner core of the Palace.

Gate of Heavenly Purity

Known as the Qian qing men this is the main entrance for the Inner Palace and during the Qing dynasty was sometimes used by the emperor for minor audiences which he conducted from a throne in front of the gate.

On the terrace you will notice two of the most impressive of the gilded lions in the palace, once again with the male lion with his paw on a globe whilst the female has her paw on a cub. There are also several gilded vats.

Palace of Heavenly Purity

Qian qing gong is the palace that faces you across the courtyard from the Gate of Heavenly Purity and is the first of the three main buildings within the actual Inner Palace. Up until the Emperor Kangxi of the Qing dynasty, the emperor lived here whilst the empress lived down the block at the Palace of Earthly Peace.

The current building is quite recent as the original was burnt down, rebuilt and burnt down again. This one dates from 1798.

As well as providing living quarters it was also the place where the emperor would hold audiences with courtiers and foreign diplomats. It was furnished with exquisite lacquerware stands, padouk wood cabinets and cloisonne braziers.

Prosperity

Also known as the **Hall of Union** this played a relatively minor part in royal proceedings although sometimes it was used as the Empress's throne room. The twenty five major seals of China were kept in special caskets inside the hall together with a small selection of treasures, the most important being a 2,500 year old clepsydra or water clock, one of China's most remarkable inventions.

Palace of Earthly Peace

As mentioned this was the living quarters for the empress during the Ming dynasty. When the Qing dynasty came into being it was converted to other purposes including, in the west wing, rooms for the practise of secret shaman rites. In the east wing a small room was used for the wedding night of the royal couple. Completed decorated in the traditional happy colour of red it proved to be more daunting than happy for the last emperor, Pu yi, who, on seeing nothing but red walls, red curtains, red bed linen, red pillows, red flowers and a bride in a red dress and with a red face, decided it was all too much and fled to spend his wedding night in another part of the palace. We assume with his bride.

To the east and west of this complex are the **Hall of Solemnity** for storing the emperor's clothes and the **Hall of Great Diligence** for the books and writing implements. Close to this latter hall is the Upper Study where the princes were taught and the South Study where the members of the **Imperial Academy** attending the emperor worked.

From here four gates in the eastern wall and four in the western wall lead to further halls and palaces. The eastern gates are Solar Perfection, Imperial Glory, Beautiful Harmony and Basic Transformation. The western gates are Lunar Glory, Splendor of the Phoenix, Intense Happiness and Proper Criteria. Considering the intrigue, war mongering and murder plotted within the Imperial Palace these names sound rather ludicrous.

Once through these gates one will find a further series of halls and palaces commonly referred to as the 'Eastern Road' and the 'Western road'. All it needs is a 'Yellow Brick Road' to compound the feeling of fantasy that tends to overcome those who have reached this far.

Eastern Road

Within this section of the palace the **Halls of Ancestral Worship** and **Abstinence** were both connected with religious traditions: the former being the **Imperial Family Temple** for ancestor worship; the latter being used for the required fasting by the emperor prior to solemn sacrifices. The nearby **Halls of Great Benevolence and Heavenly Favour** provided living quarters for various empresses and concubines.

Other halls and palaces were used as areas of study by the imperial family or for housing collections of art and books.

Symbolic of the cruel reality behind the cultured facade is a small well, easily overlooked, in a secluded courtyard amidst the myriad buildings here in the north-eastern section of the palace.

It was in this well in 1900 that the Emperor Guangxu's favourite concubine, **Zhenfei,** was drowned by the chief eunuch Cui Yugui upon the orders of the tyrannical and powerful **Empress Dowager Cixi.**

Cixi was the personification of everything evil. Upon her orders political opponents were ruthlessly eliminated. Country and friends were betrayed without thought in Cixi's dealings with the rapacious foreign powers. Family relations were exiled, executed or demoted at whim. And to feed her insatiable appetite for luxury the coffers of the treasury were emptied to the point she even diverted money meant for the Chinese Navy to pay for extensions at the Summer Palace including the construction of a giant, marble boat that could not float.

Cixi also matched her political and monetary extravagances with a gluttony that became legendary. Up to a hundred dishes would be served at a meal. Dysentery from over-eating was to be her downfall and her death followed on the gorging of herself with a gargantuan bowl of crab apples and cream.

Western Road

Cixi's power was exercised in the **Hall of Mental Cultivation** (Yang xin dian) which is situated along with other halls and the six western palaces which comprise the 'Western Road' of the Imperial Palace. As women were not supposed to be seen in public the Empress Dowager sat behind a screen placed at the rear of the throne in this Hall and from there controlled the luckless occupant on the throne in front. It was from this veiled position she compromised her nation in unequal pacts with the foreign powers.

The remainder of the western palaces and halls served as iving quarters or as centres for various, pleasurable activities: in the **Palace of Establishing Happiness** the emperor spend much time admiring flowers; in the **Hall of Double Glory** he would take tea and write poetry with palace ministers and officials.

Imperial Gardens

This is the final section of our tour of the Imperial Palace Museum.

Westerners whose idea of a garden is a strip of lawn, some rose beds and a bit of what you fancy, will be surprised and initially disappointed with the Imperial Gardens especially when seen en masse with the crowds of daily visitors.

It takes imagination and understanding of the different, aesthetic sensibilities of the Chinese to fully appreciate the subtlety and the symmetry of the garden's layout and not just see a mass of concrete paths, misshapen trees and formless rocks.

What has been created is a country in miniature with its lakes and mountains represented in the pools and many garden beds. Pines and cypresses vie with gazebos and small viewing pavilions to create an atmosphere of peace and tranquility which is very hard to capture in a visit during peak time particularly as the few public toilets in the palace are nearby along with souvenir shops. Winter, when the chill conditions keep only the bravest away, is the best time to enjoy these gardens.

Shenwumen Gate

This is the second of the two gates (Shunzhenmen is the other) by which the visitor leaves the Imperial Palace. The name is translated as the Gate of Inspired Military Genius and was separated from the interior by the rows of military barracks along the inner part of the palace walls. It was through this gate in 1644 the last Ming emperor, Chong Zhen, left to trudge up to nearby **Coal Hill** to hang himself rather than have the humiliation of handing over the Imperial Palace to the invading rebel Li Zicheng.

White Horse Pagoda

North Beijing

If Beijing could be said to have a cultural heart then north of Tian'anmen Square is where we would find its strongest pulse. Encompassing an area of parks and lakes the section immediately north of the Forbidden City includes libraries, galleries and children's recreational centres. The parks, in particular, form an escape valve for the local residents looking for the greenery they miss in the dusty, crammed streets of the inner capital.

Prospect Hill Park

This backs directly onto the Forbidden City and could well be called the 'Forbidden Park'. Like the Imperial Palace it was reserved for the amusement of the emperor, his family and close colleagues from the court. The common people were excluded from its use from the days of its creation during the Yuan dynasty (1206-1368) until 1928 (surprisingly, this was sixteen years after the public were allowed into the Palace and there appears to be no explanation for the extended ban on Prospect Hill Park).

The hill itself is not natural. When Kublai Khan, most famous of the Yuan dynasty emperors, was creating his new capital **Da du,** the earth left over from the excavations for the lakes and moats he had dredged, was used to make this oversize'd bump in the flat landscape of the city.

There have been several changes of name. When built by Kublai Khan it was known as **Green Hill.** During the Ming dynasty after being enlarged and with its base reputedly used for the storage of coal it became, naturally enough, **Coal Hill** and, under that name was the scene, as mentioned earlier, of the suicide of the last of the Ming emperors, Chong Zhen, who, according to the more lurid of contemporary accounts, fled the palace with hands dripping from the blood of the concubines he had ritually killed having earlier commanded the empress to strangle herself.

During the time of the Qing emperor, Qian long (1737-1796) a palace was built on the north side and a pavilion on the peak. Fruit trees were planted in abundance and gave the hill yet another name – Bai guo yuan or **Garden of a Hundred Fruits.** Later it was called Prospect Hill because of the pleasant views from the top, but Coal Hill is the name that still lingers on.

From the five peaks that constitute the hill the visitor can get a good idea of the layout of Beijing and the way major buildings were built along the north/south axis with the Imperial Palace as the central pivot. Of course modern day planners have ignored the ancient traditions and the east, if anything, is now the dominant architectural focal point as the majority of the high-rise, luxury hotels have been built in that sector.

If you climb up the hill from the south gate, opposite the northern end of the Imperial Palace, you will get a splendid view across the whole of the Forbidden City which gives you some idea of the careful planning and the layout of the city which can be hard to appreciate at

ground level when confronted with vast spaces and the endless series of halls and palaces. This viewpoint on Prospect Hill is known as the **Pavilion of Ten Thousand Springs.**

On the north side of the hill is the **Hall of Longevity of the Emperors** which originally contained the portraits of the various Qing dynasty emperors known as the 'Imperial Faces'. It was customary for the emperor to visit this hall with the change of seasons each year to offer sacrifices. Part of the ritual dictated he should dismount when reaching the spot where Chong zheng suicided and walk the rest of the way as a salutary reminder of what could lie in store. This Hall of the Longevity of the Emperors is a Children's Palace, a ubiquitous Chinese institution for extra-curricular activities for the brighter children.

In the shadow of Prospect Hill is Beijing's most popular park and recreation centre – Beihai.

Beihai Park

Supposedly Beihai (Northern Lake) park dates from the Jin dynasties of the 4th. and 5th. centuries. What is certain is the fact the lake, the centrepiece of this popular park, is one of three man-made lakes. The other two, the South and Central Lakes, are located behind the closed walls of the State Council compound which is the modern 'Forbidden City' being the working and living quarters for the elite of the Chinese Communist Party and off limits to the general public. The compound fronts onto Chang'an Boulevard on the western side of the Tian'anmen Gate and is so constructed that not even the open gates will reveal a glimpse into the interior due to screens immediately inside.

The park, including the lake, covers over sixty two hectares and was a handy pleasure resort for the emperors in the nearby Imperial Palace.

The onion-shaped, **White Dagoba Temple,** on the hill of the small **Qiong hua island** in the southern end of the lake, is one of central Beijing's more visible monuments.

On a summer afternoon it seems as though all of Beijing and his wife has turned out to enjoy the beauty of the park with its woods, paths and various amusements. Boating is the most popular of the recreations and some of the more daring will defy the ban on swimming.

Not everything is for enjoyment. On the northern end of the eastern side of the lake the authorities built the Young Pioneers' Hydraulic Power Station in 1956.

Qionghua Island is a magnet for visitors some of whom row out across the lake from the western shore, others using the two marble bridges from the eastern and southern shores.

Apart from the White Dagoba there are several temples and pavilions of interest and a dew-collecting dish that served the same purpose as those outside the Tian'anmen Gate. Legend tells us the Han dynasty emperor, Wu Di (140-87 BC), was told that drinking the morning dew 'from heaven' would make him live for eight hundred years. So he cast a bronze dish which he placed in the capital, Chang'an (now Xian). He must have been disappointed to find it didn't work when he turned up his toes only seventeen years after installing the dish. History repeated itself over eighteen hundred years later

when the Qianlong emperor (1736-1796) built the dish seen here in Beihai Park with the same intentions and, of course, the same result.

Scattered throughout the landscaped park are many interesting buildings. In the best condition are those of the Tranquil Heart Study found at the northern end of the western shore. Under such names as Cherish the Search Study, the Sweet-Sounding Zither Study, the Tower of Paintings, the Rippling Emerald Tower and the Fresh Green Pavilion, they form an attractive collection of rooms, all of which have been extensively renovated. It is probably fitting the Central Documentary History Research Institute makes its headquarters here in such an attractive historical setting devoted to learning.

Beihai Park also has its own Nine Dragon Screen (Jiu long bi). You will see these screens in most parts of China, many still in a state of excellent repair. They are usually six to seven metres high and about twenty metres long with nine dragons being carved on the highly glazed tile exterior to keep away the evil spirits.

This screen is close to the **Pavilion of the Ten Thousand Buddhas** which is now mute testimony to the crass, plundering of the western powers last century. The pavilion had been built by the Qianlong emperor for his mother's 80th. birthday. Inside there were 10,000 tiny gold statues of Buddha in individual niches in the walls. All these were taken by the 'foreign devils' in 1900 (it would be interesting to learn where they now reside).

Surprisingly, despite the attractiveness of Beihai park and the lake and despite being so close to the centre of Beijing it rarely pops up on city tours. It seems to be one of those places the locals like to keep for themselves. Anyway, going on your own would be much more fun than being forced to traipse round in the follow-the-leader style of group tours. There is a token fee for admittance and on a balmy, summer's evening it is the perfect spot to escape the immediate effects of Beijing's crowds, noise and pollution. In winter you can go skating on the frozen lake.

There will be no need to worry about refreshments if you get tired and thirsty. There are several ice cream and soft drink stalls throughout Beihai Park and some very good restaurants, although, if you have no Chinese-speaking guide, it maybe a case of pointing at a dish you fancy and hoping for the best.

Drum Tower

A block to the north of Beihai Park and within a short distance of the eastern shore of **Sicha Lake** is the Drum Tower which marked the heart of the earlier Beijing when it was known as Dadu and the seat of Kublai Khan in the 13th. century.

When the original tower was built in 1272 it was called the Tower of Orderly Administration. It was reconstructed just to the east of its earlier site by Yongle and had major renovations done to it in the 19th. century. In 1924 it was again renamed, this time as the **Tower of Realizing Shamefulness.**

The Drum Tower's prime purpose was as a timepiece for the city. This was achieved through an ingenious system. Four bronze clepsydras (water clocks) were installed with one being linked through intricate mechanisms with a giant, bronze gong. Through actions intitiated by the clepsydra the gong would then strike every fifteen minutes. Later, officials opted for a quieter method of time-keeping by using coils of incense that burned for two hours.

Today, of the twenty four drums which were also used to sound the time, only one remains. It shows a sword mark inflicted during the invasion by foreign powers at the turn of this century.

Correct time became especially important for the luckless court officials of the Qing dynasty. At 7 o'clock each night the ritual of 'setting the watch' took place with a two-hour interval throughout the night between the single drum beats which marked the passage of two hours. In other words, the 'first watch' would be at 9.00 p.m., the second at 11.00 p.m., and so forth. At the 'third watch' (1.00 a.m.) the officials required for that morning's imperial audience would rise. At the 'fourth watch' (3.00 a.m.) they assembled at the Wumen or Meridian Gate where they would freeze for another two hours until the 'fifth watch' (5.00 a.m.) when they were allowed into the Imperial Palace and the main courtyard, the Sea of Flagstones, in front of the Hall of Supreme Harmony where the emperor would eventually arrive fresh from a good night's sleep ready to wreak whatever havoc may be required. The 'Son of Heaven' did not take kindly to an inferior who had the misfortune not to hear the single drum beat from the Drum Tower.

The Drum tower is at the northern end of Di'anmen Road a stretch of which was known for some time as Iron Lion Lane from the pair of iron lions that stood for over 300 years outside the residence of the father of one of the concubines of the Ming emperor, Chong zhen. The lions have since been removed to the Drum Tower. This section of the road was also the scene, in 1926, of the shooting of students outside the gates of Duan Qitui's interim government – that building is now part of the Chinese People's University. The year prior, the founding father of the Republic, Sun Yat sen, had died in the same location.

Bell Tower

Sited nearby is this grey brick building which had been converted by Yongle from the main hall of the former **Temple of Ten Thousand Tranquilities** from the era of the Yuan dynasty.

There is an interesting legend concerning the replacement of the bell. The original, apparently not loud enough, was removed and in its place was hung a giant, bronze bell that was over twenty five centimetres (ten inches) thick. The legend tells how the caster of the bell, an official named Deng, had spent over a year trying to correctly cast the giant instrument and, to put it mildly, got in a blue funk when he realised the danger he was in if there were any further delays. His daughter, apprehensive at the fate awaiting her father, offered herself as a propitiatory sacrifice to the gods by throwing herself into the vats of molten bronze. Only a single embroidered slipper remained. The casting was a success and in her honour, as the **'Goddess of the Golden furnace'** a temple was built near the foundry.

Adding to the legend was the distinctive moaning sound made by the bell during high winds and storms. The sound apparently was like the chinese word 'xie' which means 'shoe', so the story was put about on those wild, dark nights that the goddess was coming back to get her slipper. This was an effective means of getting unruly children off to bed in a hurry.

Altar of Earth

Several blocks diagonally east from the Drum and Bell towers is **Ditan Park,** the site of the Altar of Earth which vies with the Temple of Heaven as the major sacrificial place outside the Forbidden City.

Built by the Emperor Jia jing in 1530 it was interesting in that the sacrificial mounds were square rather than round. This coincided with the Chinese belief the earth was square. Its construction also showed the influence of numerology as it was carefully measured in multiples of the special number six: the upper tier being 20 sq.m. or 60 'chi' and the lower tier being 22 sq.m. or 66 'chi'.

The ceremonies were held annually at the summer solstice. The emperor would spend the previous night in prayer and preparation in the **Hall of Abstinence** before making a pre-dawn, ceremonial departure for the Altar of Earth, out through the Hall of Supreme Harmony and the Wumen and Tian'anmen Gates at the south of the Forbidden City rather than through the closer Shenwumen Gate at the northern end. Possibly he took the longer way round so as to avoid going through the An ding men gate, the furthest northern gate of the main city wall, as this was the gate through which the night soil of the city was removed for treatment at the sewage farms near the Altar of Earth.

At the Altar the earth on the sacrificial mound was in five different colours representing the **cardinal points:** green for the east; red for the south; white for the west; black for the north and yellow for the centre. Here sacrifices of meat, wine and silk would be made by the emperor and echoed throughout the country with similar ceremonies offered by the highest-ranked madarin in all major provincial centres.

Although rebuilt in 1748 the Altar of Earth was allowed, in recent years, to fall into disrepair and is now mainly a public park although some remnants of the old mounds can still be seen. This is all the more surprising when you consider the attention and expense that has been undertaken to preserve the Temple of Heaven.

The Altar of Earth is normally ignored by most tourist itineraries so a devotee of history would need to make special arrangements to visit there, although it is within a reasonable hike of Tian'anmen Square.

Whilst in the area you could visit the Confucian Temple, the Imperial College and the Capital Library.

The **Confucian Temple** (Kongmiao) is from the Yuan dynasty (1206-1368) and contains a number of stone tablets listing the names of famous Confucian disciples, the list of military expeditions of the Qing dynasty and the names of the scholars who passed the triennial imperial examinations.

Immediately to the west is the **Imperial College** which was the top educational establishment in China during the imperial days. It dates back to 1287. The emperor himself would sometimes visit the Jade Disc Hall in the college to give lectures to the students and to various dignitaries.

The most important feature of the Imperial College is its collection of 189 stone tablets dating from the 18th. century and inscribed with 630,000 Chinese characters recording the Thirteen Classics. Jian Heng, the scholar from Jiangsu Province entrusted with the task, took over twenty years to complete the mammoth undertaking.

The **Thirteen Classics** comprise the following: the Book of Changes, the Book of History, the Book of Songs, the Rites of Zhou, the Record of Rituals, the Zhou, the Gongyang and Guiliang Commentaries, the Analects of Confucius, the Classic of Filial Piety, the Dictionary of Terms and the works of Mencius. The **Capital Library** is part of the Imperial College complex ranking second to the Beijing Library.

Beijing Library

Moving now over to the western side of Beihai Park on Wenjin Road we find the handsome looking buildings that comprise the Beijing Library which was constructed in several sections.

The lower, columned, triple-roofed building in front was built in 1931 whilst the higher, rear section was added in 1954. A further building was built in 1982 on the eastern side to house the computerised cataloguing and microfilming sections and additional reference and reading rooms.

Beijing Library had its beginnings in the purchase of two extensive private libraries in 1908 with the express purpose of making them available to the public.

Libraries are as old as Chinese literary history but this was the first library to be open to the general public. Strangely enough, following the official opening in 1912, the location in another, more inaccessible part of Beijing, proved to be too daunting for potential users and the library was closed the following year because of lack of readers. It was not until 1917 that it was put back into general use and following further changes of location finally settled on its present position in 1931.

An estimated ten million books are housed here with three million of those works being in foreign languages. By law, a copy of every book published in China must be lodged with the Beijing Library which also acts as a central classification centre for the 2,000 plus libraries throughout the rest of China.

The library houses a wide variety of written material. There are hand-written Buddhist scripts, Karl Marx's letters, various edtions of the works of Chairman Mao, early woodblock sets from the Song and Yuan dynasties, ancient scrolls and the Chinese equivalents of Mills and Boon.

The reading rooms can accommodate up to 1000 readers who are admitted on the presentation of a work card, student card or letter of introduction. Whilst it is difficult for a foreigner to walk in off the street and take advantage of the libraries' facilities a chat with your guide or the local office of China International Travel Service (CITS) should get you the necessary permission.

Soong Ching Ling's Residence

Moving several blocks north to 46 North River Street (Beiheyan) we find a former prince's mansion from the Qing dynasty that was converted into a home for Soong Ching Ling, a name of little relevance to the western world, but with importance within China as the widow of Sun Yat sen and as the former Honorary Chairman of the People's Republic.

In the 1960's the government restored the lovely gardens to their former glory and built a new home for Mrs. Soong which, despite a certain blandness in its government-inspired architecture, blends into a landscape that incorporates the best features of Chinese horticulture — that wonderful mingling of water, rocks and selected trees and shrubs.

Soong Ching Ling was an accomplished zither player and wrote poetry and prose and embroidered skilfully and the surroundings here reflect the cultured nature of her latter years. She died here in 1981

Yellow Temple

The Yellow Temple is the furthermost northern site within the old walled city, not far from the Andingmen (Gate of Peace and Stability).

The compound is divided into an East Yellow Temple, built in 1651 for the Living Buddha Naomuhan, whilst the second section, the West Yellow Temple, was constructed the following year basically as a residence for the Fifth Dalai Lama when he visited China. A series of small pagodas, bell and drum towers and stela pavilions complete the scene.

China Art Gallery

We now return south to the eastern side of Beihai Lake to the China Art Gallery on May fourth road. This massive, graceless building, like the museums on Tian'anmen Square, was part of the government project to build ten major, monumental edifices. There are over 6,000 square metres of floor space devoted to studios and fourteen exhibition halls.

Unless there are specific exhibitions a visit can be disappointing because of the lack of variety in Chinese art. There are not the diverse schools of thought nor the eccentric individualism that typifies western art. In artistically crude terms it could be summed up as 'once you've seen one painting, you've seen them all'. Devotees, of course, will delight in the subtle differences, but the average visitor will come away uninspired. However as souvenirs, the excellent sets of ceramic masks on sale in the Art Gallery are expensive but delightful.

China Objects

South Beijing

South of Tian'anmen Square is where you get the real feel of modern-day Beijing. Here is the wonderful, crowded chaos of the shopping district, the fascinating 'hutongs' (lanes and alleyways) and the markets.

And then there are the surprises. For amidst the noisy hub-bub you can enter a strange, underground city or enjoy tranquil gardens and the glory of the truly splendid Temple of Heaven.

Qianmen Street

Running for several blocks due south from Qianmen ('Front Gate'), Qianmen Street is the main shopping thoroughfare in Beijing although fans of the more sophisticated Wangfujing Street near the Beijing Hotel may argue differently. Certainly Qianmen is more basic, but also is more authentic because of that.

It's quite a wide street taking four lanes of traffic but gives the impression of being smaller due to the congestion. There is no such thing as a peak period traffic jam along Qianmen. It is one daylong traffic jam.

There are trees along the pavements and everywhere there are bike racks. The visitor is always amazed at just how the locals know their own bikes amongst so many exactly the same. It must work along the lines of the special 'radar' system seals use to locate their pups amongst the thousands that await their return from gathering food at sea.

You'll find the usual jumble of department stores, groceries, herbal medicine outlets, clothing shops, hardware merchants and tea rooms.

A hundred metres along Qianmen is Beijing's most popular **'Peking Duck'** restaurant, the 130 year-old **Quan ju de.** Don't expect your charming, intimate eating house. The ducks are pushed out of here on a production line basis serving hundreds of diners daily. A feature of the menu is that every main dish is from a part of the duck whether it be pickled duck's feet, duck soup or hard-boiled duck eggs. You can take pot luck and wander in on the spur of the moment but if you are in a group get your guide to make a booking. Incidentally it is not cheap. One suspects there is a 'special price' for foreigners and Overseas Chinese who are normally segregated from the main, locals' dining room.

Browsing is good fun on Qianmen but the crowds and the spitting, still prevalent despite official bans, can be off-putting.

The most interesting sightseeing in this area is in the 'hutongs' running off the major streets.

> **INFOTIP:** Unlike other Asian countries bargaining is useless within China. All the major shops are under government control and prices are fixed. It is pointless to go from shop to shop looking for a cheaper price. However with some of the smaller, private roadside shops and stalls you can still haggle to some extent.

Dazhalan Street

Dazhalan translates as 'big barrier' or 'great fence' and refers to the old curfew custom of putting a gate across the street at night to keep out intruders. There were 1200 of these dazhalans throughout the city and the Imperial Palace.

Dazhalan Street, a 'hutong' running off the top end of Qianmen Street, was the entertainment centre of Beijing during the Qing dynasty. Theatres, shops, markets and brothels thrived here as laws forbade any form of shop, theatre or noise within the Forbidden City itself.

Last century there were five major theatres in Dazhalan: the Celebrating Happiness Playhouse, Three Celebrations Playhouse, Extensive Virtue Playhouse, Extensive Harmony Playhouse and the Common Happiness Playhouse. Considering the notoriety of the red light section the Extensive Virtue Playhouse must have been named tongue-in-cheek!

One of the oldest, continuously operating shops in China is to be found on Dazhalan Street at No.24. It is the Tongrentang Traditional Medicine Shop specialising in its own lines of pills for ills since 1669. Powdered rhino horn, ginseng, deer antlers, dried herbs and snake wine would comprise many of the prescriptions made up in its back rooms. For years it was the official supplier to the Imperial Palace.

Ruifuxiang is considered the best silk store in Beijing whilst pickles and sauces are still made by the 400 year-old Liubiju store near the entrance to Dazhalan.

Dazhalan Street leads to **Liulichang Street** which is better known as Antique street because of the antique stores but actually getting its name 'Liulichang' from the glazed tile kilns that originally filled the street.

> **INFOTIP:** The Chinese government has strict regulations regarding the export of antiques. Any antique sold over the counter is unlikely to be over 125 yrs old. There will always be a red seal on the underside to authenticate its age. Any private sale outside the guidelines can result in heavy penalties for both parties if caught.

As early as the middle of the 17th. century Liulichang Street had a reputation as a centre for the scholars of Beijing who would gather here to write, to paint and to practise calligraphy. By the next century a flourishing network of bookshops and craft stores had sprung up.

Today the government has renovated and restored much of the street and the government-owned stores still sell books and old items. However there are strict controls on the sale of antiques and generally speaking artifacts over 120 years old cannot be sold for export. Approved antiques are distinguished by small red seals underneath. You won't find any great bargains nor will prices differ from elsewhere in Beijing as a fixed-price system operates in all craft shops. However the range is greater despite a deal of ordinary, mass-produced goods.

Following the destruction inflicted by the foreign forces in 1900 this interesting area of Beijing had to undergo extensive reconstruction but has still managed to retain a cluttered, vibrant atmosphere.

Temple of heaven

If you get back onto the main Qianmen Street and head south to

the second major intersection, Tiantan lu, and turn west you will be at the northern entrance to the Temple of Heaven; most tourist coaches continue down to the former city gate, Yong ding men, and park at the southern end.

After trudging through the vast courtyards, the palaces and halls of the Forbidden City, it will come as a surprise to find the Temple of Heaven, and its grounds, are actually bigger — in fact, three times as big. The deceptive appearance is because of the few actual buildings and the spacious parklands around the Temple.

Undoubtedly the Temple of Heaven (Tian tan) is the jewel in China's architectural crown. Although simplicity itself, the perfect harmony of the design, the colours and the setting lingers longer in the memory than the Forbidden city itself or even the Great Wall.

The importance of the Temple of Heaven was its position as the centre of worship to the highest deity in the Chinese pantheon, the **August Personage of Jade or Father Heaven** (see MYTHOLOGY). The major religious festivals of the year were celebrated here and such was the impact that even with the establishment of the Republic in 1912 the worshipping was continued for several years although the public were now admitted (like the Forbidden City, the Temple of Heaven had been restricted to the imperial family, high dignitaries, officials of the court and the imperial army).

The ceremonies were lengthy and undertaken with elaborate rituals and splendour.

The winter solstice rites were considered the most significant.

It commenced with the emperor and the men of the court withdrawing from the women into the **Pavilion of Abstinence** within the temple grounds. In ancient times this would be for ten days. As the years went by and the emperor's will weakened the fasting period

was reduced to three days and in the latter years of the ceremony was down to a mere overnight purge.

On the morning of the solstice the emperor would be woken several hours before sunrise to join the solemn procession to the Altar of Heaven.

No effort was spared for this procession. It was customary for elephants to be at the head, followed by musicians and singers. Then came the flag bearers carrying the banners of the twenty-eight constellations of the Zodiac, the Five Planets, the Five Peaks, the Four Rivers and so on. Dancers with peacock feathers, fans and parasols would prance along behind, just ahead of the high officials and the princes of the court. Troops of soldiers would separate each division of the procession.

Last of all would be the emperor, preceded by his exorcists. Clad in the spectacular silk robes of his office, embroidered with entwined dragons, and wearing the pearl-tasseled bonnet, the emperor would be carried in a chair so large it took thirty-six bearers to carry it.

Upon arrival at the Altar of Heaven, the three-tiered round mound in the southern section of the park, the emperor would ascend the mound and light a fire whose smoke drifting to heaven would be the invitation for the Supreme Personage of Jade to be present at the ceremony.

During the night, whilst the emperor was closeted in the Hall of Abstinence, the sacrificial animals had been slaughtered and cooked, which the cynical might think as being a particularly tantalising tease for the luckless, starving officials exposed to the aromas of roast meat wafting in from the barbecue pits.

Prostrating himself before the throne of the Supreme Personage of Jade the emperor would offer incense, rolls of silk, blue jade and finally pieces of roasted meat. This was accompanied by the singing of special hymns composed by the Office of Music who shared the same quarters as the sacrificial animals. The procedure would be repeated for each of the Ancestors and following a final, ritual nine prostrations the emperor would return to the procession and back to the Imperial Palace and, no doubt, a large banquet.

During the ceremonies the emperor would take the opportunity to 'brief' the divine one on the events of the previous year and those planned for the coming twelve months (being the winter solstice the festival was held in January or early February).

It would be fair to say the majority of visitors to the Temple of Heaven would pay little heed to the Altar of Heaven. It's just an attractive terrace of marble from which to get a better view of the **Hall of the Imperial Heavenly Vault** with its exquisite single conical roof, and the larger, triple-roofed **Hall of Prayer for a Good Year** which, naturally enough, appear to be the more important. And as the guides tend to hurry one through with a barely comprehensible commentary the lover of Chinese history would be well advised to tour the Temple of Heaven solo.

A plan of the Temple of Heaven park shows a square southern end with a semi-circular, rounded northern end; not unlike a loaf of bread.

This is part of the symbolism of the religion. The square section in the south represents Earth whilst the rounded northern section represents Heaven. Heaven was round and Earth was square in the minds of the ancient Chinese.

The philosophy of 'yin' and 'yang', the passive and active forces,

also came into play with the selection of the sites for the various celebrations. Earth, North and even numbers being 'yin', the summer solstice festivals were held at the two-staged, square Altar of Earth in the northern suburbs of Beijing whilst this winter festival was celebrated on the three-tiered, round mound in this southern part of the city. This philosophy also governed the placement of the altars, the selection of the sacrifices and the numbers involved.

So you can see there is much to ponder on when you visit this site, or any religious or imperial site in China for that matter.

Historically the Round Mound dates from 1530 a century after the buildings were completed by the ubiquitous Yong le in 1420.

From the steps of the mound you descend onto a path that takes you to the **Hall of the Imperial Heavenly Vault** distinguished by its singular, perfect cone of a roof glazed in deep blue tiles. The interior contains several altars and a wonderful view looking upwards into the inside of that cone which has been newly decorated to bring out the rich Chinese designs.

Surrounding the compound of this temple is a circular wall known as the Echo or **Whispering Wall**. It is part of the ritual of the visit to position one's self at one part of the wall and one's companion at another part on the other side of the courtyard and whisper messages which almost take on the force of a shout. Similarly if you stand on the first step at the bottom of the stairs to the Hall of the Imperial Heavenly Vault and clap or shout you will hear a single echo. Move up to the second stone and two echoes will result whilst three will be heard from the third step.

In like manner stand in the centre of the round Altar of Heaven and your speech will be echoed back to you from the marble balustrades around the terraces whilst anyone else on the platform will hear nothing. No doubt all explainable in terms of yin and yang.

Upon leaving the Hall of the Imperial Heavenly Vault there is a long, straight path called the Danbiqiao which leads to the northern section of the compound and to the **Hall of Prayer for a Good Year.**

Qiniandan

Meaning the **Hall of Prayer for Good Harvests,** the Qiniandian is the real focal point of the Temple of Heaven – certainly it is the most photographed. It somehow sums up the essence of China: the symmetry, the distinctive design, the sense of history, the very difference between East and West.

The Hall is a motivation to meditation. To sit in the shade of the cypress trees on a spring day and to just contemplate the sheer beauty of this lovely temple is what travel is all about.

However the building you contemplate is a youngster. Having been burnt down as the result of a lightning strike in 1889 it needed complete restoration. Further work has been done since the founding of the People's Republic in 1949.

The first Hall was erected in 1420 and called the Daqidian, the **Hall of Great Sacrifices.** Not one nail was used in its construction with the whole building resting on twenty eight pillars for support. There are no walls, just the pillars and a series of doors.

The pillars were arranged in symbolic circles. The centre four representing the four seasons of the year. The inner circle of twelve surrounding those were the twelve months of the year, whilst the

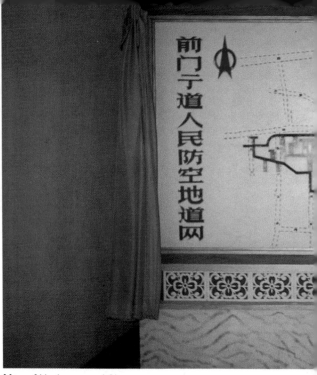

Map of Underground City

outer circle of twelve were the hours of the day, the Chinese having a twelve hour rather than twenty four hour cycle.

Set on three concentric circles of marble terraces, the three roofs of blue glazed tiles are awe inspiring. A gold sphere crowns the topmost point of the Hall.

Twice a year, the emperor would place the ritual tablets of previous dead emperors inside the Hall and offer up his prayers for a good harvest. There was not the same ceremonial pomp as at the Altar of Heaven.

There is a wonderful sense of peace and solitude here, even on days when it is crowded with tourists, which is most days. The grounds are spacious and the pleasant walks through the grassy plots and the thousands of cypress trees can be taken without interference as the visitors tend to concentrate solely on the central buildings and forget the parklands that surround the Temple of Heaven. Regrettably the quietness ends as soon as one leaves the precincts for the crowded apartments and noisy traffic intrude up to the very gates of the Temple.

Whilst the Forbidden City is the most popular attraction in Beijing, the Temple of Heaven would be the nicest.

However the most unusual would be the Underground City.

Underground City

You won't find this on every itinerary and it is not the kind of tour you can do on your own: you need permission and/or a guide. As it is not widely publicised it is wise to ask your guide or the tour desk at your hotel about a visit.

'Underground City' is actually a euphemism for the honeycomb of air raid shelters built under Beijing's streets and which link with the

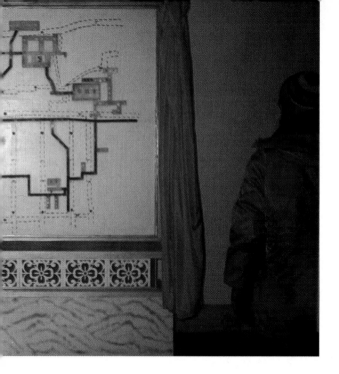

subway system to provide an extensive safety network in time of war.

The shelters were built in the 60's and 70's following the Sino-Soviet split which was far deeper than the mere ideological, family squabble the West imagined it to be. Border incidents strengthened the Chinese fear of the 'Bear' and these shelters are the result.

The entrance to the subterranean world is quite surprising. In a drapery and clothing store on a crowded 'hutong' running parallel with Qianmen Street, and only hundred metres from Tian'anmen Square, there is trapdoor behind the main counter.

Shoppers have become used to the sight of files of tourists crowding behind the counter and disappearing from sight through the trapdoor like latter-day Sweeney Todds. Steep steps take you down to the first level eight metres underground. There is reportedly another level at fifteen metres but this is not open to the public.

On the first level you will find a series of stone corridors circling, converging and branching off in a bewildering maze. These are the basic shelters with the furnished rooms that are visible being for the officials. Many thousands could be secure here but obviously not all the millions who live in Beijing. It will be a case of first come, first served or having good contacts. No doubt the staff in the drapery store above will have a distinct advantage.

With typical shrewdness the Chinese have installed a Friendship Store and refreshment rooms to cater for the daily influx of tourists.

Not only is the tour interesting but it also shows a surprising openness on the part of the Chinese. No western nation would be happy to allow visitors to wander over defence preparations of this nature.

Because of the narrowness of the corridors, the sloping floors and the flights of steps and ladders it is not a trip recommended for those with walking difficulties or those who suffer from claustrophobia. Photography is allowed by the way.

Beijing Museum of Natural History

If you have a bent for the history of the natural world then you would find this museum well worth seeking out. Hidden away in an ordinary looking building near the Temple of Heaven it is easily missed.

The museum, the first of its kind in China, is just near the northern entrance to the Temple of Heaven. Originally it was a restricted, private museum within the Imperial Palace.

Over 5,000 specimens are to be found within the three main halls of Zoology, Paleontology and Botany. They range from small scraps of fossilised seaweed from 500 million years ago to the mammoth, thirteen-metre long skeleton of the Mamenchisaurus unearthed in 1952 in Sichuan, and a mere youngster at 165 million years.

Of special interest, and useful for the traveller moving round the country, is the display of trees, shrubs, flowers and bird life of China.

Joyous Pavilion Park

Due west of the Temple of Heaven is this park inspired by the delights of drink.

Apparently it was named after a pavilion in the grounds of the **Temple of Mercy** which bore an inscription taken from an ode by the Tang dynasty poet **Bai Juyi**: 'Let us wait until the chrysanthemums are golden and our wine matured, then all shall be intoxication and joy'.

Although it is now very attractive with its man-made lakes and islands, for many years it was a dank, unpleasant haunt for criminals and suicides. Restoration work since 1952 has changed the park into a pleasant retreat.

Links with the history of old Beijing have been retained including the place where the Republic's founder, Sun Yat sen, organised political meetings. There is the **Fragrant Tomb** where, legend relates, many citizens, rebelling at the Manchu orders to change their Ming dress after the fall of the Ming dynasty, hid their robes. There is also the **Parrot Tomb** which is supposedly the burial place of the pet parrot belonging to the Qing calligrapher Deng Wanbai who even wrote a poem upon its death at the hands of a cat.

The two big archways you will see here once graced the eastern and western sections of Chang'an Boulevard before widening of the road necessitated their removal. Other archways, temples and pavilions add to the appeal of the park which provides a handy refuge from apartment life for the locals who live in this southern section of the city remote from Beihai Park in the northern suburbs.

Ox Street Mosque

Ox Street, in the southwestern section of Beijing, about ten blocks to the west of the Temple of Heaven, is a stronghold of the **Hui people,** the second largest of China's minority nationalities with a population estimated around four million. Of course they don't all live in Ox street, being scattered through the major regional areas of

China but this section of Beijing has always attracted large numbers of resident and visiting Hui.

It also attracts large numbers of Moslems both from the Hui people who belong to the Islamic faith and also from local and foreign Moslem visitors.

The name 'Ox' refers to the Islamic preference for beef and the taboo on pork unlike the other Chinese in the district, especially the dominant Han race who often chided the Hui over their religious and racial differences.

The Ox street Mosque is the oldest and biggest of the mosques in Beijing which are believed to number over eighty. The original temple was built in the early part of the Song dynasty (960-1279) and constructed along purely Arabic lines. Subsequent restoration work as recently as 1955 added more Chinese characteristics to the architecture.

Nasruddin, a 10th. century Arabic preacher, was the inspiration behind the mosque's construction, so naturally the main chambers face towards Mecca.

Inner courtyards, gardens, minarets and Arabic decorations add a distinction and variation to this house of prayer that makes it unique amongst its neighbours, such as the Temple of Heavenly Peace a few blocks to the north west.

Temple of Heavenly Peace

This mustn't be confused with the Temple of Heaven.

Although the oldest, extant building in Beijing the Temple of Heavenly Peace didn't achieve the imperial importance of the Temple of Heaven.

The current pagoda dates from about the same time as the Ox Street Mosque although there had been an earlier pagoda on the site nearly four hundred years prior.

Traditional design includes an octagonal tower the height of a thirteen storey office block making a change from the many shorter, rounder temples that abound in Beijing.

It is not necessary to make a special trip to inspect the Temple of Heavenly Peace, but if in the area and you feel in need of your daily 'fix' of temples it is worth visiting.

East Beijing

The city and inner suburbs east of Tian'anmen Square represent the 'up market' end of Beijing. Fanning off from the eastern section of Chang'an Boulevard you will find the best shopping, the top luxury hotels and the diplomatic quarter. Unfortunately you also get those interminable rows of faceless apartment buildings which is why the stunning hotel complexes stand out like chopsticks at a barmitzvah.

Beijing Hotel

Regrettably when it comes to looks the venerable Beijing Hotel is no match for the likes of the newer, flashier establishments such as the Sheraton Great Wall, the Kunlun or the Shangri-la. The service doesn't exactly overwhelm you either (the Beijing's lobby lounge will grudgingly serve you the worst sandwiches in creation!). But as the first hotel to cater for the international trade and with an interesting history behind it, the Beijing retains an exotic aura that puts it in the same legendary category as Hong Kong's Peninsula, Bangkok's Oriental or the Manila. When old 'China hands' get together to reminisce it will certainly be of the Beijing Hotel and not of any of the modern upstarts.

With 900 rooms spread over three wings that range from the ugly to the more ugly to the even uglier, the Beijing, like Topsy, has just 'grow'd'.

Before the turn of the century this prime site on Chang'an Boulevard, within a short walk east of Tian'anmen Square and the Forbidden City, was occupied by the Military Garrison Headquarters. As China moved into its post-Imperial era the headquarters were pulled down and the first of the the hotel's buildings, the central seven-storey wing, was erected. This was known as the' Grand Hotel de Pekin' reflecting the French financing and management. This remained the case until 1940 when the Japanese took over and called it Riben Julebu (Japan Club).

The western block of the hotel was opened in 1954 with a twenty year gap before the largest of the wings, in a style that could be called 'Sixties Motel', was opened to the public in 1974. This eastern part of the hotel now serves as the main entrance whilst the grand doors in the central section seem to serve either as a formal entrance for VIPs or for tradesmen – I suppose being a workers' state, there should be no difference. There have been three major renovation and refurbishment programmes in recent decades.

The lounges and lobbies of the Beijing Hotel seem to be the main rendezvous points for businessmen, diplomatic staff, weary shoppers and bug-eyed tourists. However, apart from officials and hotel staff you won't see any local chinese who are obviously discouraged. For visitors there are money changing facilities and excellent souvenir shops.

Wangfujing Street

Wangfujing Street is to Beijing what Fifth Avenue is to New York. It is the capital's top shopping avenue. That's where the resemblance ends for here, on this narrow thoroughfare running north along the side of the Beijing Hotel, there are no skyscrapers, no Tiffany's, no fancy boutiques. But in terms of crowds and enthusiasm there is just as much fun shopping here – and you won't need an overdraft to settle your bills.

The name 'Wangfujing' is a derivation from 'Wangfujie' which meant **Prince's Mansions Street** so called as the emperor, Yongle, in 1417, built ten mansions in this area to provide high class accommodation for the major, hereditary princes.

Later the word 'jing' or 'well' was added since there was a natural well on the site now occupied by the office of the People's Daily newspaper. A natural well was extremely beneficial as a monopoly on the sinking of wells was retained by the imperial court as it was considered any unplanned alteration to landscaping could affect the well-being of the emperor and his family. Good fortune was closely linked with 'fengshu', which means 'wind and water', and necessitated the careful positioning of any building to take best advantage of the correct and most propitious 'fengshu'. Even in as sophisticated city as Hong Kong building of those fantastic office blocks and hotels will not go ahead until the correct 'fengshu' has been ascertained.

Wangfujing Street's prosperity came with the founding of the Republic in 1912 which saw the top end of the Chinese social scale, the bureaucrats, the politicians and the high military officers move into homes in this eastern section of the city. To cater for their expanding tastes and revenues shops selling luxury goods such as furs, western clothes and antiques soon started to appear along this muddy track. As with any bureaucracy it was not long before the road which they had to use daily was soon paved. At this time it was also known amongst the foreign community as Morrison Street.

Today's visitor will find a fairly narrow road but with broad pavements and the various stores set well back.

The major store is the **Baihuo Dalou,** the Beijing Department Store. Several storeys high it is a rather gloomy store due to a general policy of dim lighting and dimmer service that is normal in Beijing shops, with the exception of Friendship Stores. Clothes are the main lines carried on the ground and first floor and to western eyes will appear rather drab and unfashionable; to the Chinese they represent the height in desirability. On other floors you will find household goods and the usual range of tourist-style souvenirs.

There tends to be a sameness about the shops mainly because so many have set their sights on the tourist market offering a similar range of porcelain mementoes, jade carvings and bracelets, calligraphy sets, decorated eggshells and superb glass and crystal perfume bottles which have been painted from the inside – an exquisite and fascinating craft, but the bottles do not come cheaply.

Well patronised are the small fast food stalls with non-stop sales of soft drinks, ice cream, boiled corn cobs, steamed buns and chinese 'shaslik' sticks.

Wangfujing Street is open seven days a week and whilst the weekends are the busiest times you will never find it empty during shopping hours, generally 9am to 7pm, although smaller shops have more flexible hours than the big stores.

The immediate area around Wangfujing Street has its own history with the names of the streets and lanes reflecting the activities that were once part and parcel of life in Beijing and which, unfortunately, have died with the past.

Lantern Market Street, going back to the Ming dynasty, was the main place to buy lanterns in Beijing. The traders would hang lanterns from poles along the street both for sale and for decoration. In winter transparent ice lanterns were made, being a specialised craft at the time. The market also sold a wide range of goods including luxury items like furs which sold well amongst the Chinese elite who lived in the district.

Annually there was a major lantern market which took on the atmosphere of a festival attracting visitors from all over the city and from the outlying districts. The ritual of the lantern market was conducted until the early part of this century when the turmoil of the Boxer Rebellion and the invasion by the foreign powers put paid to many of the old traditions.

There are still some lanterns to be seen in nearby shops but most are mass-produced and there is very little evidence of a major cottage industry.

Close by, on the western side of Wangfujing Street, is the efficient Capital Hospital which has an excellent department dealing with eye problems. Also in this area is **Nai zi fu Lane,** or Nurses' Office Lane, which recalls the days of the Ming dynasty when wet nurses for the imperial babies were lodged in this quarter. Twenty wet nurses were kept on permanent standby and it was customary for those who had just given birth to a girl to be given a prince to nurse and vice versa.

Mongolian Banquet

Several streets up is **Eastern Factory Lane** or Dong chang hu tong which gave the name 'Dong chang' to the infamous secret police of the Ming emperors, who had barracks here.

About a kilometre north-west is the **Dongsi Mosque** which dates back to the early 15th. century being then known as the Temple of Purity and Truth which apparently was a common name given to all mosques in China. The current buildings have been extensively renovated over the past forty years. Foreign Muslims living in Beijing use this mosque for their devotions and ceremonies. The **Dog Temple,** dedicated to the dog of the Tao mythology figure, Er lang, is within a few minutes walk of the Dongsi Mosque whilst also nearby is the **People's Market,** today nothing like the original with its stalls temple complexes and narrow lanes. However it is worth wandering round the present market site and the modern-day shops, restaurants and cinemas catering for the local population rather than the foreign residents and the tourist trade as on Wangfujing Street.

Up until recently there were several old survivors of the ancient craft of bow and arrow making. At the height of the Qing dynasty there were fifty families living in a section here called Bows and Arrows Courtyard where they produced these weapons of war for the imperial armies and any freelance adventurer who came to town.

Friendship Store

Inevitably if you visit Beijing you will end up at the Friendship Store A stop there is on every package city tour, hotel courtesy coaches use it as a set down and pick up point and it is a ready reference spot for meetings amongst the expatriates who use the supermarket section for their weekly shopping.

The Friendship Store is located at 21 Jianguomenwai which is the eastern extension of Chang'an Boulevard and is about two to three kilometres from Tian'anmen Square. Every taxi driver in town knows its whereabouts and most east/west buses pass the door.

The building is functional rather than decorative and inside can be a bit confusing with strange corridors leading to the most unlikely places. You almost need a guide map to find the supermarket section.

The supermarket is an excellent spot to stock up on western food items if you are suffering 'knife and fork' withdrawal symptoms after too many battles with chopsticks and glutinous rice. The prices are high. Being right next door to the diplomatic compounds the management shrewdly capitalise on the extensive 'hardship' allowances diplomatic staff have and which they spend with great gusto on the imported food items and liquor. If you are headed for inland China it is worth getting a few items to tide you along especially in some of the more remote areas where the hotel catering deteriorates in direct proportion to the distance from Beijing.

Although prices are high in the imported food departments they are remarkably cheap elsewhere, especially for locally made clothes. Whilst not particularly stylish the prices are so low that for everyday, round-the-house wear you could have a field day. The padded jackets and coats filled with goose down are amongst the best buys along with lengths of silk and cotton materials, blouses, shirts and cashmere sweaters.

There is a large selection of porcelain, chinaware, jade and precious stones. Imitation Tang horses, only marginally smaller than life size, compete with awesome jade and ivory sculptures of breathtaking size and workmanship.

Leather jackets are there in abundance however the styling and manufacture are rather crude.

A book section stocks some first rate maps and guides to the city and to China plus a selection of foreign magazines and newspapers including daily editions of the South China Morning Post to supplement the meagre ration of overseas news in the English-language China Daily.

If you don't like crowds then try and avoid the Friendship Store on Saturday afternoons when most of the foreign residents do their shopping. There are other Friendship Stores in Beijing but this is the largest and most comprehensive. Incidentally there is no bargaining and you can be assured of good quality but indifferent service: a smile from the shop girls is as rare as a portrait of Chiang Kai shek. Unlike western cities there is no point in shopping around as all prices are fixed throughout the country with the exception of the small, free-enterprise shops.

> **INFOTIP:** Foreign tourists are issued with a special currency which is negotiable only in the major shops and Friendship Stores. However, smaller establishments and markets will often accept this but your change will be in the common Chinese currency which cannot be exchanged for your own currency when leaving the country. Only the official tourist money will be converted back on your departure.

Jianguo Hotel

A ten minute walk from the Friendship Store past the depressing apartment blocks of the lower end of the diplomatic compound, running a gauntlet of currency changers and beggars, will get you to the Jianguo Hotel the first of the new breed of hotels to be built in Beijing.

Reputedly based on the design of a Holiday Inn in California, the hotel is managed by the Peninsula Group from Hong Kong and so introduced a new set of standards for the hotel industry. It is not as impressive as the more recent high-rise palaces that hog the skyline but there is a pleasant intimacy and less tendency by the staff to take themselves too seriously.

After the rigours of shopping it is worth the walk up to the Jianguo to get a cool beer or iced coffee in the lobby lounge and to use the toilets which don't advertise their presence with the same vile aromas so prevalent in the Friendship Store.

Ritan Park

If you care to walk north through the leafy streets and the pleasant homes of the diplomatic compound where large gardens, tennis courts and swimming pools are in sharp contrast to the grey, crammed streets of the workers' quarters, you will come to Ritan Park a block away from the main Jianguomenwai Street.

This is the site for the **Altar of the Sun.** Although accepted as gods, Sun and Moon worship was not deeply ingrained in the general religious thinking of the people but was practised mainly by the emperor. Sacrifices were only made every two years, during the odd numbered years for the Sun (yang) at this altar and during the even numbered years for the Moon (yin) at a similar altar in the western suburbs.

The ceremonies would take place at sunrise in Spring and at sunset in Autumn and would follow the general format used at the Temple of Heaven i.e. ritual sacrifices of animals (an ox, a sheep and a pig) and offerings of wine and coloured silk and jade (red for the Sun, white for the Moon). Music, singing and dancing would accompany the emperor's prayers.

Flower beds, parklands, man-made lakes and hills now provide attractive pleasure gardens where the altar once stood.

Beijing Ancient Observatory

This symbol of one of China's finest, oldest and most highly developed sciences is almost lost amidst the trappings of the new.

On Jianguomenwai, on the opposite side west of the Friendship Store and where the walls of the old capital Dadu once stood, the ancient, weathered bronze globe and dragon screen that adorn the roof of the observatory are now tucked away in a fold of overpasses and expressways so as to be almost inconspicuous.

Work on the observatory began in 1437 at a time when China was becoming more adventurous and her ships were venturing further out into the oceans of the world. The observatory was to help in plotting navigational charts with a secondary, but equally important purpose of establishing a stronger base for the astrological predictions that governed life in China for so many years.

However it was not always the exact science the emperor wanted in those days. Muslims took over the observatory but then lost control to the Jesuits who had moved into the country following the evangelism of Matteo Ricci at the start of the 17th. century and proved to be more accurate.

The Jesuits in a case of religious one-upmanship predicted an eclipse and this so impressed the emperor he handed over the running of the observatory to them. The Jesuits also established a meteorological station in Shanghai.

Many of the instruments were looted by the French and Germans in the wake of the Boxer Rebellion and the foreign intervention that followed but were returned under the terms of the Treaty of Versailles in 1919.

Renovation work was undertaken to strengthen the observatory tower following demolition of the city wall and subway construction in the 1970's. It is now open on a limited basis to the public daily except Monday. It is worth noting that many of the opening hours for public monuments and buildings can be quite arbitrary and some unforeseen holiday or sheer contrariness can mean there is no admission just on the day you intend to visit. It's wise therefore to check with the hotel tour desk or CITS before making what could be a fruitless trip.

Beijing Railway Station

Talking of fruitless trips many a traveller has come unstuck at Beijing's Railway Station. The incredible growth of inbound tourism, antiquated booking procedures and a little corruption on the side has seen hundreds of passengers stranded without valid tickets for train travel.

A major crackdown by authorities revealed alarming numbers of ticket scalpers who, through contacts in booking offices, were buying bulk tickets and then holding seatless passengers to ransom with their high prices.

Beijing Railway Station is situated on Chongwenmen Dongdajie a block south of Jianguomenwai and approx. one kilometre south west of the Friendship Store.

It's very much a case of beauty being in the eye of the beholder. To the average person it is just an extremely large barn: crowded, noisy and confusing. To the train buff it is close to paradise because this is one of the few main stations in the world where you can see steam trains. Admittedly they are getting fewer and fewer with the introduction of featureless diesel trains. However, as Datong, on the Trans-Siberian line some eight hours to the west of Beijing, is the last city in the world to be making steam engines (although rapidly scaling down) the joys of smoke, cinders and screaming whistles can still be had here. However you will possibly see more steam engines in the industrial section of the outer western suburbs.

The Beijing Railway is also a terminus for the subway system (the **'underground dragon'**) which is everything the above ground station is not. It is neat, efficient, fast, economical, clean and impressively decorated.

West Beijing

Walking along Chang'an Boulevard west from Tian'anmen Square would lead you eventually into the western suburbs which straggle out for some thirty kilometres into the Western Hills. This is the older, less developed part of town with fewer of the impressive freeways that slice through the eastern section and with more of the older apartment buildings and homes. But it is also the gateway to important attractions like the Great Wall, the Ming Tombs and the Summer Palace. But within closer proximity to the Forbidden City there are several historical sites and recent additions worth considering.

South Lake

Nanhai, the Chinese translation of South Lake, is the southern extension of the three lakes lying just outside the western walls of the Forbidden City with the North Lake forming the basis for the well patronised Beihai Park.

Unfortunately the South Lake is not so accessible. Indeed you could say that having liberated the original Forbidden City the authorities decided to replace it with their own version which is the series of buildings, temples and pavilions surrounding the waters of the South Lake and which now house the residences and offices of the Central Committee of the Communist Party and the State Council. A depressingly dull fate for a part of Beijing which, from all reports, is one of the loveliest areas in the central district.

As early as the Liao dynasty (907-1125) the gentle hills and small pools here were attracting the imperial court who used to stroll and take their pleasures.

With the greedy acquisitiveness that is the hallmark of all authority it was only a matter of time before one of the emperors had the bright idea of enclosing the land for the exclusive use of the court. This happened during the time of Kublai Khan when the capital was known as Dadu. Not only was the area seconded to the Imperial Palace but the lakes were widened and the dredgings used to construct what is Prospect Hill. The walls were further extended by Yongle in 1417.

Chang'an Boulevard is the southernmost border of this complex of parks and buildings which is now known as the Zhongnanhai Compound.

Walking west on Chang'an Boulevard along the broad pavements in front of the Tian'anmen Gate you'll cross a small but busy street, Nan Chang jie bei, which runs north under the walls of the Forbidden City. From this street the high red wall of the Zhongnanhai Compound stretches for a full block west effectively secluding the interior and its inhabitants.

The main gate onto Chang'an Boulevard, **Xinhuamen** (China New Gate) is not for the likes of you or me, nor for the ordinary Chinese. It is the official entrance for the highest dignitaries and visiting firemen. Others on official business use an entrance on Nan Chang jie bei which also provides an entrance for those wishing to visit Chairman Mao's former residence which is the nearest the average person will get to the official compound.

You won't even get a glimpse of the inside through the main gate as a large screen, emblazoned with a red star, together with armed guards have been carefully positioned so that any view is completely hidden. The People's Government, like its imperial ancestors, can be very elitist.

There is a delightful, romantic legend attached to the main gate, Xinhuamen. During the time of the emperor Qianlong (1736-1796) he built a special marketplace and mosque, both in the Islamic fashion, for his favourite Muslim concubine to relieve her homesickness. **Perfumed Consort,** for that was her name, would go the gate tower

to look across to the market and the mosque which reminded her of her homeland and so the gate became known as the Gazing Home Tower.

Less pleasant stories about the compound attach to the infamous 19th. century **Empress Dowager Cixi** who not only had her nephew, the weak-kneed Emperor Guangxu, exiled to the Sea Terrace Island in the middle of South Lake, but also had the many elm trees in the area destroyed after a caterpillar fell from one of the elms and had the temerity to bite her.

Sea Terrace island was popular with the emperors especially during the hot, dusty summers. A quick but ceremonial journey next door gave them respite from the heat and the claustrophobic rooms of the Imperial Palace. It was common practise to rule for most of the year from the South Lake.

A small plot of ground in the **Garden of Plenty** was used for 'rehearsals' for the annual ceremonies at the Altar of the God of Agriculture some distance away. This involved the emperor in some physical labour. He was required to plough a strip of earth as part of his devotions before the Altar and to make sure he could plough a straight furrow he would practise in these gardens.

Also in the Garden of Plenty is the former home of Chairman Mao which has become a museum of homage though not quite on the scale of his mausoleum in nearby Tiana'men Square. The rooms have been kept as he left them with various personal mementoes and collections of his works.

Although not publicised to foreigners the home is open to the public on a limited basis: generally on the third Saturday of the month. It may be possible for groups to get special permission to enter at other times but this would depend on the mood of the authorities at the time.

Cultural Palace of the Minorities

The Cultural Palace of the Minorities is on Fuxingmen Street, the western continuation of Chang'an Boulevard the change of name coming at Xidanbei Street, several blocks from Tian'anmen Square.

Built in 1959 the three wings of this large complex act as museum, library, restaurant and relaxation centre for the 53 'cultural minorities' who comprise 7% of the Chinese population (the other 93% being of the Han race).

The building was fashioned after the Chinese character for a mountain which looks like a Roman 'w' with an extended middle prong. This centre section is thirteen storeys high and towers over the eastern and western wings which are three storeys each.

Entrance into the white marble foyer of the central hall is through giant bronze doors bearing the chinese symbols for 'progress' and 'solidarity'. Huge relief decorations depict the minorities and the areas from which they come.

For the tourist the most interesting section will be the museum which is housed in the central tower. The various exhibits are spread through five main exhibition halls backed up with displays in the maze of smaller rooms.

Similar formats have been used for all the minorities' displays depicting ethnic and geographical backgrounds, political activities, liberation movements and recent achievements. To fully comprehend China it is necessary to appreciate the place Minority Peoples occupy in Chinese society and their importance in the eyes of the Government. These displays go some way to increasing one's understanding provided they are not viewed solely through rose-coloured (red) glasses.

The serious scholar wishing to study the subject in more depth could apply to use the library in the basement to the north of the main entrance. The library holds up to 600,000 books and the extensive material on the minorities together with a wide selection of localised newspapers and magazines will provide fertile field for research.

The east wing contains an auditorium and studios with facilities for radio and television broadcasts. The western wing houses restaurants, dance halls and meeting rooms. There are more restaurants in the central tower with an observation floor at the top of the building which gives excellent skyline views across central Beijing.

Next door is the Minorities Hotel which is reserved for visitors from the various autonomous regions although other guests have been admitted in the peak tourist seasons when pressure on the city's hotels is acute.

Southern Cathedral

Before we leave this general area if you are interested in seeing the oldest Catholic church in Beijing then retrace your steps a hundred metres or so to Xindanbei Street, cross over Fuxingmen and head south for several blocks until you come to Cathedral of the Immaculate Conception at 18 Qianmenxidajie.

A church had stood here in the middle of the 16th. century but the the founding of the cathedral did not come until 1650 when permission to construct a larger church was given to Father Adam Schall. Schall had taken charge of the fledgling Catholic community following the death in 1610 of the famous Jesuit missionary Fr. Matteo Ricci who had lived and worked in a house on the site.

It was fifty three years before the actual cathedral was completed and one of its distinguishing features was the **Virgin Chapel** where,

in deference to Chinese custom, women prayed separately from the men. This segregation lasted up until this century.

During the early part of the last century, due to conflicts between the emperor and the Church, the cathedral was largely uninhabited and for two decades was only saved from demolition due to the watching brief of the Russian Orthodox bishops who preserved the church and its library until a French order of priests were able to take over in 1861.

Earthquakes damaged the building in in 1775 and then flattened it in 1900. The present building was erected in 1904 but without the panache of the earlier cathedral.

It is still an active church and although the local Chinese clergy have not found favour with Rome it still functions as the headquarters for the Chinese and expatriate Catholic communities. A public Mass is celebrated on Sundays and feast days.

Military Museum of the Chinese People's Revolution

Of all the museums possibly this is the most relevant for modern-day Chinese for it charts the foundation and progress of the People's Liberation Army without whom there would have been no successful Revolution.

The Military Museum stands on the main Fuxingmen Street three to four kilometres from Tian'anmen Square and one of the last major buildings before you disappear into the wilderness of the western suburbs. Set back from the road amidst rows of identical apartment blocks and similarly large government buildings it is easy to miss. However the 'heroic' statues of soldiers in the forecourt and a giant Red star on the facade are a dead giveaway.

The architecture follows the standard format: a large central block with two smaller wings. The spacious forecourt with revolutionary statues, fountains and pools adds an impressive note that would otherwise be lacking. The unmoving, unblinking sentries would put the guards at Buckingham Palace to shame for sheer immobility if somewhat lacking in spit and polish.

Inside, the Revolution is charted with a fulsome display of photographs, charts, maps, weapons and memorabilia. A certain amount of artistic license has been taken with the paintings which fall into the mould of 'Heroic Socialism' beloved of Eastern bloc countries and which bear as much resemblance to reality as Picasso.

The various eras of the Revolution have been divided between different floors in the museum and together form a comprehensive history of the years from the founding of the Chinese Communist Part in 1921 to the declaration of the People's Republic in 1949. Admission charge is minimal.

Yuayuan Lake and Angler's Terrace

Behind the Military Museum is another of those delightful parks and lakes that continue to surprise one in Beijing.

The name 'Yuayuan' means Jade Pool although in previous generations the lakes and its surrounds were commonly referred to as the Angler's Terrace after a 12th. century official who lived in seclusion here disguised as a fisherman.

Fishing had been a popular pastime for members of the imperial court and the nobility for centuries. As far back as the 4th. century emperors would take their leisure by the lake which is fed with ever-flowing streams from the western hills.

The last emperor, Pu yi, gave the park as a gift to one of his teachers. Shortly afterwards the area fell into neglect. Eventually the terrace and remaining pavilions were restored and in 1956 the Government dredged a new lake, diverted water from the Yongding River to fill it, landscaped the grounds, built new bridges and rockeries and finally erected a state guest house, Diaoyutai (Angler's Terrace).

Altar of the Moon

The eastern exit of Yuayuan park will lead you towards the Altar of the Moon. There will be no difficulty finding the site as a television tower stands there.

As referred to earlier when discussing the Altar of the Sun, moon and sun worship did not dominate the public's religious practises having more the aura of a cult reserved for specific worshippers including the imperial household.

The emperor would make his annual sacrifice at the autumn equinox normally in the early evening. A pig, an ox, a deer and a sheep would be offered up together with white jade and white silk.

unfortunately it takes a great stretch of the imagination to bring these rituals to mind as the temple area is now the province of a school and a sports ground as well as the television tower. However the terrace and some of the stone porticos are still standing.

White Dagoba Temple

A kilometre to the north east of the Altar of the Moon, and easily recognisable, is the White Dagoba Temple situated on Yangshidajie (Sheep Market Street). It is a larger version of the temple in Beihai Park and is part of a monastery complex going back to 1096. Originally called the Temple of the Emperor's Longevity and Peace it was given its present name, Miaoyingsi (Divine Retribution), when a new temple was built in 1457. The dagoba is the largest structure of its kind in Beijing being taller than its counterpart in Beihai Park.

The distinctive beauty of the dagoba is due largely to the design of

Three Gorges

the 13th. century Nepalese architect, Arnico. When he died he was given the honorary title of 'Duke of Lianguo' by a grateful emperor.

The White Dagoba is considered a classic Buddhist temple and is noted for its collection of Buddhist religious artifacts, paintings, sculptures and prayer wheels.

Major repair work had to be undertaken following damage caused from the tremors of the 1976 Tangshan earthquake and during those renovations workmen unearthed hidden Buddhist scriptures, religious icons, jewellery and bronze images of Buddha. Stones reportedly taken from the ashes of Buddha's cremated remains were also found.

During the excesses of the Cultural Revolution the temple was temporarily used as a factory but a return to reason at the end of this turgid period saw a restoration to its rightful museum status.

The dagoba's distinctive look is gained through a girdle of thirteen bands which are referred to as the 'Thirteen Heavens'. Thirty six bells hang from a bronze disc near the peak of the conical spire whilst a small, bronze pagoda perches at the top.

Having seen the dagoba in Beihai Park you may not feel like making a special journey to this dagoba but if in the area make the effort, particularly if you have a basic knowledge of Buddhist worship and the symbolism of their sculpture.

Lu Xun Museum

Lu Xun, the pseudonym of Zhou Shu ren, is regarded by both Chinese and Western critics as the finest modern writer this century with no peer during his lifetime nor since his death in 1936.

Placed on a pedestal by the Communist Government, surprisingly he never joined The Party, indeed, shortly before his death the writer expressed doubts about the party machine: 'Once a person goes inside the Party he would be bogged down in meaningless complications and quarrels'. Lu Xun's appeal was a strong social conscience

combined with an eloquent style and a passion for the proletariat.

Born in 1881 Lu Xun grew to manhood during the dying days of the last imperial dynasty whose court was rife with corruption and murder instigated by the ruling Dowager Empress, Cixi, who had sold out the Chinese birthright to the foreign powers. Intrigue, greed and social inequality preyed on the mind of the young writer who initially had gone to Japan to study medicine.

After seven years in Japan Lu Xun returned to China in 1909, became a schoolteacher, joined the Ministry of Education, lectured at Beijing University, translated Russian stories, wrote his first work 'Diary of a Madman' (1918) and then in 1926, as leader of the 'literary revolution' (League of the Leftist Writers of China) and in company with other radicals, fled Beijing for Shanghai. Here he allied himself with the communists and anonymously wrote various political tracts attacking Chiang Kai shek whose followers sought to assassinate him. But for all his political activity Lu Xun's fame was won on his literary merit. In a rare step for a Chinese writer he absorbed western philosophies and through his stories translated them to the Chinese scene whilst still retaining a distinctive Chinese character. His work could never be dismissed as derivative. It was wholly personal.

Lu Xun's interests were wide and this museum, which is close by the home where he lived from 1924-1926, displays a representative selection covering such diverse works as his translations of the novels of Jules Verne, notes for botany lectures, political tracts, documents, Russian novels and a collection of Tang and Ming antiques.

The museum, which is in a lane off Yangshi dajie not far from the White Dagoba Temple, is a modern building and therefore of little interest except for the mementoes it contains. The home, however, is a good example of a typical Chinese house of the time. It is a basic quadrangle design with the apartments, studies and kitchens surrounding an inner courtyard with a further small garden at the rear. Guides will probably claim several trees there were planted by Lu Xun himself. Actually they were replanted in 1956!

Beijing Zoo

We've moved half a dozen blocks north west to a section that contains the Beijing Planetarium, an indifferent Exhibition Centre and the Beijing Zoo.

Most zoos are depressing and pointless and this is no exception. It is built on land that alternated between imperial and private ownership.

In 1906 an experimental farm and zoo was created and opened to the public in 1908 under the name **Garden of Ten Thousand Animals** which was more than a slight exaggeration. Only now does it have anything approaching that number.

Most westerners will head straight for the Panda enclosure which is scruffier than the animals themselves (Chongqing in Sichuan Province has much better conditions for these cute animals). There are Manchurian Tigers, Pere David deer, golden monkeys, various cranes and kangaroos.

There are nearly 7,000 animals and 600 different species. Considering the Japanese poisoned most of the animals in 1937 with the laughable excuse of protecting them from air raids, the collections shows a deal of hard work has gone into building up the Zoo.

Beijing Planetarium

This is of fairly recent construction having opened in 1957 with its huge dome making it a local landmark in the north western suburbs. It is opposite the Beijing Zoo.

If you have seen other planetariums you will know what to expect. There are halls with exhibitions of photos and charts of the heavenly bodies and a circular auditorium where regular 45 minute shows are given. Most of the old astronomical instruments are at the Ancient Observatory near the Beijing Railway Station.

Five Pagoda Temple

This temple was specially built by Yongle in 1473 to house a series of golden Buddhas and a model of the Diamond Temple at Bodh Gaya in India's Bihar State where Buddha traditionally was supposed to have received enlightenment.

Unfortunately enlightenment was not a quality of the foreign powers who, in 1900, successfully completed the looting of the complex which they had begun in 1860.

Most of what remained was sold off piecemeal by the squabbling factions of the central Nationalist Government in 1927. Still the excellent temple with its five pagodas has managed to survive and has been restored with its wonderful Buddhist carvings and Sanskrit writing.

Outskirts of Beijing

Despite the many wonderful sights to be explored within Beijing proper – the old walled city limits – many would argue the more spectacular attractions are outside the inner city area. And that would be an argument hard to fault when you consider the Summer Palace, the Great Wall and the Ming Tombs, all of which are 'musts' if you are visiting China for the first time.

More and more travellers now visit these monuments independently but the newcomer unfamiliar with Beijing would be wise to take one of the daily package tours or at least hire a car with a guide/chauffeur. This will take all the worry out of negotiating the crowded, confusing streets and the guide's knowledge of the history and important features of the monuments is usually extensive.

> **INFOTIP:** Taxis are readily available. It is easier to get taxi at one of the major hotels than by hailing in the street. For longer trips, say to the Ming Tombs, the Summer Palace or the Great Wall where it is essential the taxi waits for you, it is advisable to negotiate a flat fee either with the driver direct or, if his English is non-existent (more likely than not), through the hotel taxi desk or concierge.

Summer Palace

Of all the places where the Imperial court took its leisure this would be the most charming and the most relaxing. In fact, one can easily understand why the infamous Empress Dowager Cixi happily diverted funds intended for the Imperial Navy to improve and extend the Summer Palace although she did go a touch overboard with the building of the ridiculous Marble Boat.

We have **Wan Yanliang,** the first emperor of the Jin Dynasty, to thank for the Summer Palace. Back in 1153 he was so taken by the delights of the wooded hills and the placid lakes he ordered the construction of the first palace shortly after moving his capital to the Beijing area. On what is now known as Longevity Hill he built his 'Gold Mountain Travelling Palace' and despite a name that sounds like a fugitive medicine man from America's Old West it was apparently quite impressive.

Although Wan Yanliang called the hill **'Gold Mountain'** it was later changed to the more prosaic **'Jug Mountain'** in honour of a legendary jar found inside a rock there. The jar was of great beauty and full of rare treasures which were removed by the old peasant who had found the jar. But the old man decided to leave the jar on the hill and before he departed inscribed the sides with the words ' When this earthen jar is moved, the emperor's decline shall begin'. Now this wouldn't be a good legend without an appropriate ending. Sure enough, when the jar disappeared during the reign of Jialing (1522-1566) the emperor's reign ended and eighty years later the Ming dynasty collapsed. This would have happened anyway, but why let facts get in the way of a good story.

Wan Yanliang was responsible for diverting the Jade Spring and the resulting waters filled the lake he named the 'Gold Sea' and which is now **Kumming Lake.**

Further emperors extended the lake or diverted streams to increase the water capacity, the last one to do so being the 18th. century Emperor Qianlong who employed over a hundred thousand workers to deepen and widen the lake to the size it is today. He renamed the lake Kumming after Kumming Lake in the old Han dynasty capital of Chang'an where the Emperor Wu Di used to hold naval exercises.

The Summer Palace was then linked with the Forbidden City by a series of canals along which the emperor would be rowed in a waterborne ceremonial procession whenever he changed residences for the summer.

Various temples and halls were added by the emperors such as the Temple of Gratitude and Longevity which Qianlong built to celebrate the 60th. birthday of his mother. The park was then called Park of Pure ripples (Qingiyuan).

It present name, Yiheyuan, **Garden of Good Health and Harmony,** was given by Dowager Empress Cixi who, in 1888, spent several fortunes (money designated for the Chinese naval forces) on reconstructing and enlarging the Summer Palace following the wanton destruction by the English and French Forces during the Opium Wars. The only structures not destroyed by fire at the time were the bronze pavilions and the stone pagodas.

The Summer Palace was destroyed again by foreign forces in 1900 and once again Cixi poured an endless amount of cash into its rebuilding. Whilst it was certainly unbridled extravagance for those days the legacy as a result of Cixi's rampage with the cheque book is a truly wonderful vindication. Undoubtedly she did not have posterity in mind, just her own gratification, but let's be thankful for her persistence in re-creating the Summer Palace.

True to form there was also a dark side to Cixi's interest in the complex. The luckless Emperor Guangxu, formerly locked away on Sea Terrace Island in the South Lake next to the Forbidden City, was transferred here by Cixi and imprisoned for ten years until his death in 1908.

Upon the founding of the Republic, after the Revolution of 1911, the Summer Palace became the private property of the Last Emperor, Pu Yi, who then opened it to the public for the first time in its history. However the entrance fee was so steep the public stayed away in droves.

After Pu Yi left the Forbidden City the government turned it into a state-run public park and from then on the Summer Palace went into decline. The treasures were looted by the Kuomintang when they fled China for Taiwan and the Japanese occupation added further devastation. From 1949 onwards large-scale restoration work has been carried out and the result is splendid.

An estimated two million visitors a year flock to the Summer Palace which is eleven kilometres north west of Tian'anmen Square in the **Haidian district.** On a summer weekend it seems as though the whole two million go there at the same time, therefore the best course is to try and make your tour of the grounds on a weekday.

The main entrance is through the gates in the eastern wall and the exit is normally through the north palace gate after following the traditional walking route through the palace grounds. You can do it in reverse which means walking against the tide and on a busy day it is best to go with the flow. Anyway the tourist and city coaches all stop at the eastern gate so you don't have much choice anyway. As it gets

positively chaotic in the car park it is a wise idea to make a note of your coach's number and position. Should you miss the bus getting transport back to central Beijing is difficult because of the lack of taxis and the lack of comprehensible English signs on public buses. The best alternative is to hitch a ride with one of the other package tours even if it means slipping the other guide and driver a few yuan each.

The entrance at the eastern gate is through a large wooden 'pai lou' or ceremonial archway. Just inside the 'pai lou' is a map showing the outline of the palace grounds and is in both Chinese and English. The long, dusty forecourt is lined on either side by souvenir shops, refreshment stalls and toilets. The toilets within the Summer Palace are not conspicuously marked in English but can be distinguished by their smell. Ladies take note! There is no Western-style seating: the toilets are flush to the ground, pun intended!

Immediately ahead is the **Eastern Palace** Gate guarded by the now familiar, traditional pair of lions. In the centre of the flight of stairs leading up to the Gate is the normal marble slab, carved with entwined dragons, for the carriage of the emperor. There is also a **'spirit wall'** to keep out unwanted evil spirits and unwanted guests, not unlike the large wall inside the southern entrance to the government residences and offices at South Lake, next to the Forbidden City. The small murky pond and its two marble bridges, just past the 'spirit wall', was once the sole province of the Imperial family during the days of Cixi.

Hall of Benevolence and Longevity _____

We come now to a second paved forecourt which leads to the first of the major pavilions, the Hall of Benevolence and Longevity which, until 1890, was the Palace of Encouraging Good Government obviously dedicated to one of life's more impossible tasks!

A series of bronze animals in protective wire cages stand in the forecourt including deer, a unicorn and cranes.

Large incense burners in the shape of turtles and filled with sand also decorate the spacious courtyard.

Despite the courtyard's size it quickly becomes crowded as the local guides use the area to lecture their groups in front of the hall on the general history of the palace. Take care as it is very easy to join the wrong group and many a tourist has wandered off blindly following the wrong flag.

There is also a small pool beside the steps to the hall which is used as a 'wishing well' into which the Chinese throw small coins.

Inside the Hall of Benevolence and Longevity is a hardwood throne and, until recent times, a screen from behind which Cixi pulled the strings of the puppet emperor on the throne. Considering the nature of the woman and her utter contempt for moral and legal niceties, this deference to the ancient Chinese tradition of women being neither seen nor heard is odd, to say the least.

It is possible, unlike the Forbidden City, to enter this chamber and walk the corridor that runs behind the throne. A series of windows reveal tiny rooms used for living quarters with the beds immediately striking one as being incredibly small and uncomfortable. An otherwise attractive, decorative mirror behind the throne has not stood up well to the passing of time and is pitted and showing marked deterioration of the silvered backing. The chandeliers are extremely 'kitsch' in their brightness and gaudiness, which is quite surprising in a country which was a leader in the subtlety of the decorative arts. Another unusual feature are the two enclosed models of underwater scenes standing on either side of the main door. The scenes are contained within table-like structures on high legs. In fact they were used as tables but with a difference: under the glass tops were large fish tanks and rare goldfish would swim through the carefully created models for the amusement of the court who would dine or conduct their business on the top of the tank.

One can also walk around the Hall of Benevolence and Longevity and view the interior from the outside. However, as the windows seem to be washed only irregularly it is a little like peering into a blank television screen.

Several metres to the north of the Hall of Benevolence and Longevity is the Palace of Virtue and Harmony.

Palace of Virtue and Harmony _____

This three-tiered structure in dark stained timbers was used as a theatre and for all the world reminds one of early prints of the theatres at the time of the Bard. It is very 'un-Chinese'.

The theatre occupies one section of a courtyard with surrounding buildings supplying excellent vantage points from which the court could watch the various productions. The actual stage was larger than normal and was on three levels. Upon Cixi's annual arrival on April

15th. (she would stay until October 15th.) and on her birthday the same opera was simultaneously performed on the three levels giving one three times as much enjoyment or, for that matter, three times as much boredom. Cixi herself would take part in some of the stagings.

The theatre was equipped with sophisticated features for that time. Trapdoors in particular were popular with openings in the ceiling of the lowest stage and further traps in the stage floor itself. Characters could thus drop from the sky or emerge from the underworld as the script demanded. Large tanks under the theatre were filled with water pumped up from Kumming Lake and would be used to provide clever underwater effects.

Theatregoers needed great stamina as many of the performances would go on for days with the Empress Dowager watching from a throne in the opposite building.

In the adjacent courtyard is the **Hall of Jade Ripples,** the prison-home of the Emperor Guangxu who is said to have worn away impressions in the flagstones with the incessant tapping of his walking stick at the frustration of his imprisonment.

Garden of Harmonious Virtue

A short walk up the hill in a north easterly direction, almost retracing one's steps, leads to one of the most peaceful and beautiful parts of the Summer Palace. The Garden of Harmonious Virtue is perfection in miniature.

A series of small pavilions linked by paths and covered walkways spill around a tranquil pond covered with lotus flowers. Often called the 'garden within a garden' it is a faithful reproduction of the famous Jichang Garden in Wuxi in the eastern Jiangsu Province.

The peace and the serenity have an instant soothing effect and very few people visit the Garden of Harmonious Virtue without spending a few minutes sitting and contemplating the gentle scene. Even on the busiest day at the Summer Palace the garden is an oasis, miles away from the noise and throngs.

Hall of Joyful Longevity

Situated on the north bank of Kumming Lake the selection of chambers that comprise the Hall of Joyful Longevity provided the living quarters of the Empress Dowager Cixi.

Dining room, bedroom and small offices are grouped around a courtyard with its sprinkling of magnolia and flowering crabapple trees. It is rather appropriate there are crabapples here as the fruit was one of the Empress' favourites and the trigger for her demise. Cixi was renowned as being a glutton and at a meal would pig out on anything up to 128 dishes which left her a victim of constant dysentery. Her undoing came with a huge bowl of crabapples and cream after which the Imperial body revolted and gave up the ghost. In season you can get crabapples in toffee which are sold in small clusters on a stick at a refreshment stall half way along the Long Corridor. It seems as a appropriate a souvenir as any postcard or engraved mug!

The position of the Hall of Joyful Longevity is most pleasant with a long and broad southerly aspect of the Kumming Lake.

The Empress had her own private jetty attached to her living quarters so when she arrived by boat she would dock at her very front door.

Kumming Lake

So much extending, dredging and re-coursing work has been done on Kumming Lake it may as well be considered man-made.

Occupying three-quarters of the total area of the Summer Palace it is an integral part of the whole harmonious look.

Most of the buildings and features of the palace have been designed to take advantage of views of the water with the complex spreading itself along the northern shoreline in the lee of Longevity Hill.

About three hundred metres south of the Hall of Joyful Longevity is the Seventeen Arch bridge stretching in graceful curves for 150 meters out into the Lake to join with Southern Lake Island on which is the **Temple of the Dragon King.**

The **Seventeen Arch Bridge** itself is a delight. The five hundred balusters (the short supporting columns to the balustrades) are each decorated with carved lions in differing poses. On the shore, at the

entrance to the bridge, is a massive bronze ox. Chinese custom required a cast of an ox to be placed near any completed work done on a lake, river or other water system. The ox was to represent man's mastery over the water and, hedging the bets, as a protection against flooding.

The bronze ox is one of the few extant objects in the Summer Palace from the days of Yongle. Being of bronze it weathered the fires lit by nature or invading forces and being so heavy was ignored by the looters who were looking for more portable booty.

Slightly north of the ox is a tall tower dedicated to the God of Literature.

After crossing the Seventeen Arch Bridge which is sometimes known by the more romantic name of The Bridge of Embossed Ripples, you will come to the Temple of the Dragon King. This is a Taoist temple and is dedicated to the dragon who controls the waters of the Lake. Obviously the ox was not considered powerful enough to deter the dragon.

An extended embankment across the lower southern third of the lake acts as a causeway with the **Jade Belt Bridge** being the link to the western shore. The Jade Belt Bridge is noted for the lovely marble carvings of cranes in flight. A tall pagoda on a hill on the distant southern bank completes the landscape that looks as though it was designed by an artist.

In winter when the lake freezes over and mists rise from the iced surface there is a special charm about Kumming Lake. Of course the absence of crowds helps one to more fully enjoy the chilly beauty of the scene.

Summertime brings an entirely different picture into view. The Chinese love the water, dragons or not. And whilst a great number swim in the lake the majority are content to hire the small rowboats and that's cause for amusement all round. Being urbanites and without ready access to the ocean the seafaring skill of the average resident is about zero. Oars in particular appear to give great trouble and your Sunday rower soon finds out that a 'crab' when rowing is a different kettle of fish to the one he finds in his favourite seafood restaurant. It is not uncommon to see the odd boat and its occupants upended into the lake causing more mirth and merriment than concern.

The less adventurous will take one of the sedate rides in the ferry boats that cruise along the lake at regular intervals. Recently the ferry boats were upgraded and the rather drab, unpainted vessels have been replaced by bright and colourful **'Dragon Boats'** although nothing like their sleeker namesakes which are used in the traditional Dragon Boat races.

The shores of the lake are a favourite picnic spot and although noisy and crowded on a hot summer afternoon the western visitor will be impressed by the good manners of the locals who know how to enjoy themselves without undue horseplay at the expense of others. However the dreaded 'ghetto blaster' is starting to make its presence heard.

The Long Corridor

For many visitors the Long Corridor is possibly the outstanding feature of the Summer Palace (Changlang).

Corridors, or covered outdoor walkways, have always been an important feature of Chinese gardens especially where they border a pond or lake.

The Long Corridor is the daddy of them all; at 728 metres it's the longest one in China and possibly the longest covered walkway in the world. It runs along the northern shore line of Kumming Lake at the foot of Longevity Hill.

The structure, which dates from the end of the 19th. century, is a reconstruction of the original corridor built in 1750. The crossbeams effectively divide it into 273 sections with the ceiling of each section, along with both sides of the crossbeams, being painted with scenes of Chinese landscapes, flowers, birds, animals and various legends, some quite gruesome and violent, others with a touch of humour — in one scene a character even seems to be indulging in the ancient practise of 'mooning'.

During the Cultural Revolution fanatics had many of the scenes painted over so as to discourage the people from believing in 'legends'. These paintings have been restored and have a slightly different quality to them than in the original form. Anyway most of the decorations have been renovated in recent years so don't expect a 'weathered' antique look to the corridor. To study each painting separately could take days as there are over 7000 different works with over 300 historical stories illustrated.

The Chinese have a romantic tradition that if a young couple start walking together at the start of the Long Corridor by the time they have completed the 728 metres they will be engaged.

The corridor has low railings so the elderly or infirm can take a rest if the walk seems too long. There are also two kiosks serving soft

drinks, ice cream and, in season, toffee crabapples on a stick.

On the lake side of the corridor there is a path skirting the shoreline like a quieter service road running parallel to the busy motorway. Shaded by willows and cypress trees it is pleasant to lean on the marble balustrades and watch the activities on the lake.

On the land side Longevity Hill towers above dotted with forests and various temples which can be reached by long flights of steps up the hill. There are also several restaurants serving passable Chinese food but as they are extremely popular a booking is advised. An alternative is to take a picnic lunch; this is the ideal place for that.

INFOTIP: Most traditional Chinese festivals are celebrated in a low key, personal fashion, if at all. On the other hand the major political events, e.g. May Day, Founding of the Republic, become the subject of gigantic parades. If it can be arranged it is worth timing your trip to coincide with such a celebration for the sight of Tian'anmen Square packed with people is something to treasure.

Hall of the Parting Clouds and the Marble Boat

At the halfway mark of the Long Corridor there is a slight bulge in the shoreline which was obviously man made with an eye to the symmetry of the landscape. On the lake side there is a pavilion and a refreshment kiosk whilst on the hill side steps lead up the Hall of the Parting Clouds.

This is a charming collection of pavilions with a lotus pond in the central courtyard. **The Empress Dowager Cixi** had expensive renovations done and used the chamber for her birthday celebrations which saw all the courtiers, including the emperor, prostrate themselves before her.

Also pandering to her ego is a large portrait attributed variously to American and Dutch painters, but 'Old Masters' they were not. The portrait was painted when she was well past the 'three score years and ten' of our allotted span but the artist painted her as a thirty year old woman to placate her self esteem.

Behind the **Hall of the Parting Clouds** are steps leading up to the Hall of Virtuous Light and behind that, the furthermost building on Longevity Hill, **the Pagoda of the Fragrance of Buddha.**

Over sixty metres in height, the attractive pagoda is considered to be the finest piece of architecture within the Summer Palace. Buddha himself must have been pleased with the temple and the superb view over the glazed tile roofs below and the shimmering waters of Kumming Lake.

Back at lake level the Long Corridor finishes near the ferry boat terminal, you turn the corner and immediately you have the most useless water craft in the world – the Marble Boat. Built from naval funds appropriated by Cixi it sits there at its own jetty unable to float. The boat is not completely marble: the hull is, but the upper structure is wood painted with a marbled effect. The wily Empress, who was often called 'Old Buddha', would dine here with specially constructed mirrors suspended from the walls in front so the trusting soul could see the reflection of anyone behind her.

The path from the Marble Boat winds past a rusting old steam vessel, the gift of a European monarch, and past several shops selling herbal remedies but nearly always closed. You can then exit the palace via the north gate or take a climb up through the cypresses on Longevity Hill. This track leads to the splendid **Long Bridge** curving gracefully over **Suzhou Creek** providing wonderful views through the magnificent ceremonial arches up to the Pagoda of the Fragrance of Buddha as seen from the rear northern face of Longevity Hill. This area around the Suzhou Creek is being developed as a tourist resort with hotels and parks.

Ming Tombs

It seems to be an indelible part of the human psyche that one must remember the glories of one's life with appropriate monuments after death. Those who achieve greatness, or even have it thrust upon them, are destined to be commemorated with grandiose post-expiation reminders. From the pyramids of the pharaohs to the Italianate frippery of Hollywood's Forest Lawn the rich and famous don't feel secure underground unless something weighty and impressive is on top.

The Chinese emperors were no different (nor even socialist emperors for that matter; witness Chairman Mao's elaborate mausoleum in Tian'amen Square).

The various dynasties, depending on where the court was located at the time, had themselves put to rest with appropriate pomp and splendour. And for that we can be thankful as their funereal rituals and burial sites have proved to be fascinating attractions for the tourist and to have historical interest as well.

Undoubtedly the most famous and most spectacular burial site of all is that of **Qin Shihuang** at Xian in Shanxi Province, with all those incredible, life-size, terracotta warriors and horses.

By comparison the Ming Tombs are disappointing with little to see within the tombs. However they are of historic value and the scenery is pleasant.

The Chinese name is 'Shisanling' from 'Shisan' for 'Western Hills' and 'ling' for 'mound' or 'tumulus'.

The tombs are fifty kilometres north-west of Beijing. You follow the main road to the Great Wall turning off at the village of Changping which is four kilometres from the entrance to the tombs which are situated in an area spreading over forty square kilometres of valley and lower slopes of the surrounding mountains.

There are thirteen imperial tombs scattered around the site which was carefully chosen to satisfy the requirements of 'fengshui' (wind and water) which needs the right balance of the elements to ensure good fortune.

Here the hills provided protection from the worst of the winds coming across from the deserts of Mongolia and the slopes are gentle enough to ensure the proper drainage of water.

The tombs actually date from the third Ming emperor, Yongle, as the first, Hongwu (founder of the Ming dynasty) built his tomb at **Nanking**, the capital at the time, and the second, Jianwwen, left no trace whatsoever.

The first indication of the approaching Tombs is a fourteen metre high marble archway. This is a rare example of Ming stonework having been built in 1540 during the reign of Jiajing. It is in excellent condition having escaped the despoilation of invading forces and being far enough out of Beijing to avoid the corrosive effects of pollution. The five archways are supported on pillars whose bases are covered with fine bas-relief carvings of lotus flowers, lions and dragons. In olden days the funeral procession would pass through the main archway.

Further along the road is **The Great Red Gate** which leads you into the Sacred Way or Way of the Spirit stretching for seven kilometres to the actual tombs. There are three grand archways almost forty metres high with the central archway reserved solely for the passage of the dead emperor's body. Living members of the imperial family used the other archways. The ordinary people were left out in the cold; they were completely forbidden to enter the region.

Next is the **Stele Pavilion** which has, reputedly, the largest stele (inscribed slab) in China. Erected in 1426 it is ten metres high and is mounted on the back of a tortoise which symbolises the universe: the shell is the sky and the underneath is the earth.

Then we come to the most impressive avenue lined with large stone carvings of various animals. There are twenty four in total. Twelve are standing showing they are 'on duty', whilst those 'off duty' are kneeling down. The animals comprise lions, elephants,

camels and mythical beasts in twelve pairs. The animals serve as omens and as potential aids in the afterlife.

A bend in the road, deliberately made in the interests of 'fengshui', reveals a further guard of honour, this time human. There are twelve figures of high mandarins from the government and military service. Each one, by the way, is sculpted from a single piece of stone.

Beyond this is the **Dingling tomb.** Whilst there is no restriction on visiting the other tombs in the area the tourist is always taken to this particular resting place which once housed the remains of the **Emperor Wanli.** What was left of him, amounting to some bones and hair, has been taken away. Considering the advanced nature of early Chinese civilisation it is surprising there was no development of mummification as in Egypt.

Wanli chose the site for his tomb in 1583 when he was only 22. It took six years to build, employed vast numbers of artisans and workers and cost an imperial fortune (an estimated eight million ounces of silver). Whilst there were several exterior buildings, many damaged during various invasions, the main chamber was deep in the earth so the tomb has been called the **Underground Palace.**

Excavation work on the tomb was done in 1956, a singularly difficult and exacting job in itself because of the intricate system used in sealing the tomb. However the Chinese are renowned for their patience and their skill as archaeologists as the painstaking reconstruction of Xian's entombed warriors shows. Similarly the Dingling tomb is a masterly example of their care and thoroughness.

The approach to the tomb, situated at the foot of Dayu Mountain, is via two courtyards flanked with rooms used either as museums or souvenir and refreshment shops.

The museums contain a photographic record of the excavation work plus funerary objects, various ornaments and costumes, coins and decorative head-dresses.

Separating this front section of the complex from the tomb itself is Fangcheng which means 'Square Tower' although sometimes it is referred to as the 'Soul Tower'. The tower is part of a wall circling the large burial mound and called the Precious Citadel which you need to climb before tackling more steps into the tower. Surrounded by penci pines and cypresses it is an attractive front to the tomb entrance which, unfortunately, is rather depressing.

As the tomb is twenty metres underground you need to reach it along a sloping concrete tunnel with the inevitable souvenir sellers and their stalls lining the walls of the tunnel.

Within the tomb itself there is another section of tunnel leading to the emperor's burial chamber with two other burial chambers for the empresses forming underground wings. Stone doors of gigantic proportions can be swung across to seal the chambers. An ingenious system of suspended stone blocks could be activated to swing into position from the inside effectively preventing any entry from outside which is why the modern-day excavation work was so cleverly done. According to stories handed down there were other secret tunnels which led to exits in the nearby hills and the workmen who constructed them were killed to prevent the details being made known.

Killing was very much part of the burial rites. Various concubines would be buried alive so they could serve the emperor in the other world. Their tombs are separate from the main mausoleum.

Inside there is very little to see. Like the pharoahs' tombs the Ming Tombs were once repositories of great treasures and from the Dingling tombs alone over three thousand objects were removed after the excavations. All that is left are several marble resting places for the coffins, some attractive pottery jars and vessels used in the funeral rites, and some large, empty, red lacquer boxes.

The original contents showed a careful selection was made to provide the imperial rulers with plenty of luxuries in the next world.

Fine silk robes, golden crowns, suits of armour, swords and other weapons, sedan chairs, cosmetics, bowls, chopsticks and fine porcelain all shared entombment with the emperor. Many of these articles recovered from the tomb are now on display in the museum halls in the forecourts.

The largest and finest of the Ming Tombs however is **Changling,** that of emperor Yongle. This is quite fitting when you consider Yongle was responsible for so many of the splendid ancient buildings within Beijing proper.   Changling is largely above ground and is on the southern slopes of the hills. It is entered through a triple-arched Gate of Eminent Favour which leads to the Hall of Eminent Favour in front of the 'Precious City', a circular wall surrounding the burial mound.

The scope of the burial site shows that neither money nor imagination were stinted in its preparation. The vast courtyards, the large Hall of Eminent Favour with its great pillars, the impressive archways and the hillside surroundings with the specially planted pine trees testify to a man who went out as grandly as he lived.

Paper Dragon maker

The Great Wall

'A man is not a man until he has walked the Great Wall', Chairman Mao.

Whether Mao actually said those words is debatable but they are blithely trotted out by the guides to justify a trip to the Great Wall. Not that any justification. The majority of those coming to Beijing for the first time would have this at the top of the list.

The fact it is also the only man-made object visible from the moon has become something of a cliche you only half believe.

When confronted with the Wall's sheer grandeur, and there is no other word to describe it, the cliche becomes reality.

At times it is hard for the mind to take it all in. To stand on the Wall and to see its immense size is to wonder at the splendid imagination that spawned a fortification so awesome and so effective.

One tends to revert to Ancient Egypt for comparison and look at the Great Pyramids for confirmation that Man can raise to great heights of inventiveness whether keeping away the living or protecting the dead.

Visitors will find it an uplifting experience although Somerset Maugham, upon viewing the Great Wall and recording his thoughts in his 1922 book 'On a Chinese Screen' uses the phrase 'silent and terrible', a reference to both the physical presence and to the history of the Wall which was built with blood cementing the stones together.

Countless thousands of men died during its construction. Prisoners and conscriptees laboured in brutally hard conditions driven to collapse by the ruthless Imperial builders.

Naturally legends developed out of their travail. A simple story,

embellished by time, soon took on mythical proportions. Such is the tale of **Meng Jiangnu.**

Meng Jiangnu's husband was forcibly conscripted to work on the Wall. After years of separation and with no word from the husband, Meng set out on the difficult journey to the Wall to find him. Further long months of searching revealed no trace. Resting one day on a portion of the Wall she could no longer contain herself and burst into floods of bitter tears. Tears fell like rain upon the stones and were of such strength this section of the Wall actually crumbled. As the stonework fell apart it revealed the corpse of the long lost husband; upon which the unhappy widow drowned herself in the sea.

The fanciful embellishments of the legend notwithstanding, the very real suffering forced upon the ordinary people is well illustrated in that story.

Although parts of the Great Wall can be seen at various spots throughout China the bulk of tourists will visit it at **Badaling,** 70kms. north west of Beijing. Here the Wall is relatively modern, mainly of the 14th. and 15th. century origins.

But China has been building Walls since as early as the 6th. century BC. With all that practise it's no wonder they have the job down to a fine art!

The Great Wall had its start in the 5th. century BC during the period of the Warring States.

Cities and villages had sprung up on the Central Plain of China and the inhabitants found they were at the mercy of the nomadic tribes from the north whose fleet horsemen and archers, like all guerilla forces since, made swift forays into the populated areas without warning, wreaking whatever havoc they felt like wreaking and then just as swiftly retreating to their own homelands.

As a result a motley selection of unrelated walls appeared in the states of Yan, Zhao, Wei and Qin who used their mountain ridges to erect primitive defences.

Two hundred years later, following his subjugation of the different states, **Qin Shi Huang,** the first emperor of a united China, had these 'bits and pieces' of walls linked together as one unifying defence system rather than the disorganised collection of ineffectual barriers reaching out in differing directions.

300,000 men then toiled to extend this early chain of walls into the basis of the single, long construction we know today. This early wall stretched for 6,000 kilometres starting at Liaodong in the north, encompassing the Gobi Desert and finishing further south at Lintiao in Gansu province.

The passage of time and frequent battles took their toll and the original enterprise soon found itself in ruins.

In 1368 the first of the Ming emperors, Zhu Yuanzhang, took on the task of reconstructing the Great Wall and over a 100 year period it was restored. Basically it followed the original direction and measurements but with some variations. It runs for 6,000 kilometres from the Jiayu Pass in the west to the Yalu River in the east.

In China it is often called the Ten Thousand Li Wall, a 'li' being approximately five hundred metres. In truth it should be called the Twelve Thousand Li Wall.

Side Road Snack

Travellers headed for Badaling to visit the Great Wall have a choice of two methods — by rail or road.

The train, which leaves the main Beijing railway station, takes a little over two hours and it is a relaxed way to see urban Beijing and the nearby rural districts. You are deposited at Nankou station and proceed the extra kilometre on foot or by donkey.

Nankou (Southern Pass) was an early stopping place for the caravans on their long trek to Mongolia. It was a bustling, fortified town of inns and markets of which there is little evidence today, except for the bustling part.

By car or coach the road branches to the left at Changping (the Ming Tombs are to the right). The old two-lane road carrying traffic in both directions has been upgraded for the latter part of the trip and is now a separated highway which has considerably shortened the time of the journey.

Approaching Nankou, either by rail or road, the flat rural landscape changes to mountain passes with tiny stone cottages, well camouflaged amidst the rocky terrain, grimly hanging onto the side of the hills. A few chickens scratch desultorily in the dusty earth and the snort of pigs in their pens can be heard on the clear air. The living looks as tough as the countryside. At least the heavy tourist traffic gives the opportunity for roadside stalls.

Winding down the slopes of Nankou Pass there is a 'subsidiary' wall; not part of the Great Wall but an additional defence. Some will mistake this at first for the main wall but the size will soon correct that impression.

The Great Wall comes into view with an impact that is not lessened by the fact you are awaiting it. The closer you get the larger it becomes but to appreciate its size one needs to climb onto the Wall itself.

The entrance gate (there is an admission charge) is a few metres from the road which narrows to a one way track to pass through the Wall.

After running the usual gauntlet of souvenir shops and kerbside photographers there is a nifty climb up the steep steps onto the broad top of the Wall. Actually it is like a small road and can hold up to five mounted horsemen which was the builder's intention.

Approximately seven metres wide the Wall is eight metres high. Because of the many hills in this region the sinuous curves of the Wall skirting the ridges provides a dramatic sight.

Should you be there in a winter the spectacle is even more awesome with the white snow contrasting against the brown stonework. And there is the pleasant bonus of having the Wall to yourself unlike Spring and Summer when the sightseeing becomes a battle against a moving ocean of people. It is advisable, as with most attractions in Beijing, to opt for a weekday visit to avoid the weekend rush of locals.

Once you climb the wall there is a choice of two directions. To the left is the steeper path and even with guard rails to cling to it can be very tough going for those short of wind or limb. The Wall to the right is easier although it has its share of steep, slippery inclines.

Towers and parapets provide plenty of opportunities to stop and admire the panoramic views of the mountains and the valleys to the west.

On the other side a township of shops and restaurants has sprung up. The range is quite surprising. You can buy cheap, poorly made T-shirts with lurid sketches of the Great Wall or at the other extreme very expensive and finely crafted carpets. Jewellery, ivory and jade carvings, decorated chopsticks, porcelain and thick, fur-lined hats can also be purchased. The restaurants are ordinary and you will have to pay a minor fee to use the toilets.

Purists might quibble about the shoddy, ramshackle cluster of shops but it does add a quaint bazaar-like atmosphere. The Great Wall has survived worse than this.

The Western Hills

Being within ten to fifteen kilometres of downtown Beijing these lovely wooded hills are a popular haven for the locals who seek the coolness and shade in Summer, the solemn solitude in Winter and the remarkable colours in Autumn and Spring.

The Western Hills are in close proximity to the Summer Palace so the two are easily combined for a pleasant day's outing.

The most favored part is that section known as **The Fragrant Hills** or Xiangshan Park, 1600 hectares of hills, streams and forests renowned for the glorious autumnal tonings of the Huanglu or **'Smoke tree'** which is actually the Hungarian fustic.

In the 12th. century, during the time of the Jin dynasty, this was a

Kumming Lake

regular hunting haunt for the imperial court. The Jin Emperor Xiang Shizong built the Xiangshan Temple which served as his palace and as a hunting lodge.

By the time the 18th. century arrived the game had been hunted out so the the Emperor Qianlong surrounded the area with a wall and imported Manchurian deer. Apart from this distasteful practise he was also responsible for erecting numerous pavilions, pagodas and archways and changed the name to Jingiyuan or **Garden of Peacefulness.** There were twenty eight different components in Qianlong's architectural and landscaping plans which turned the park into one of the loveliest and most imaginative in China. The 19th. and 20th. centuries, with the decline of the Qin dynasty and the frequent incursions by foreign powers, were not so kind and the buildings were destroyed or fell into disrepair whilst the beautiful gardens faced a similar fate. Since the arrival of the People's Republic in 1949 restoration work has done a lot to rectify the situation and it is certainly worth the time if you are looking for a mental and physical break from the normal pace of life in modern Beijing.

The name, Fragrant Hills, is a slight misnomer. It should be Incense Mountains from the name given to two large rocky outcrops on **Worried Ghost Peak,** the 560 metre hill which is the highest point in the park. When the mists form around the peak and the outcrops there is a resemblance to an incense burner, hence the reference.

It is possible to climb up the track to the top of the **Incense Burner**

Peak or you can use the cable car. It takes about an hour by foot. The locals often call the peak the 'Devil's Frown'. From the top there are excellent views across Beijing. In fact the park is one of the selected sites spread through the city known as the 'Eight Views'.

Temple of the Azure Clouds

At the north eastern end of the Fragrant Hills Park, as a sort of dog-leg addition, is the Temple of the Azure Clouds on a sloping hillside part of the Western Hills.

Built in 1330 it was originally a convent and called the Nunnery of the Azure Clouds. The buildings reflect both the Indian and Chinese architecture with the former well represented by the **Diamond Throne Pagoda** noted for its central design surrounded by various stupas.

Although they did not see the ironic humour in the situation, a group of rich 16th. century eunuchs tried to convert the nunnery into an ornate mausoleum for their eventual burial. This idea, although started, never reached fruition.

Major renovation work and new construction was undertaken two hundred years later by the Emperor Qianlong who was responsible for the erection of the Diamond Throne Pagoda.

As with many of the sites around Beijing it was allowed to deteriorate (either through neglect or active destruction) during the latter part of the last century and during this century until after 1949 when the new nationalism that swept the country manifested itself in major reconstruction of historically important locations.

Today the Temple of the Azure Clouds is a most attractive complex. Possibly the most outstanding feature is the collection of 508 gilded wood replicas of **Lohans,** or Buddhist saints, in the **Hall of the Immortals.** This is spectacular, not only for the number involved, but also for the sheer individualism of each statue. Attitudes and facial expressions are all different.

Similarly fascinating is the **Temple of the Sleeping Buddha,** a short walk away, through the gnarled old pines and cypresses. Here you'll find this wonderful five metre-long statue of Buddha reclining on his side cast from 250 tons of copper and surrounded by painted statues of Buddha's twelve disciples.

In complete contrast is the museum to the Republic's founder, Sun Yat-sen, to whom a Memorial Hall is devoted.

Upon his death in 1925, for unexplained reasons (there seems to be no historical link with the Temple) the Leader of the Revolution was buried here at the base of the Diamond Throne Pagoda until 1929. The body was then transferred to Nanjing and his hat and some of his clothes were buried in its place (well, they do say 'clothes maketh the man'!). The memorial halls have a display of photographs of his career, various quotations from The Works, a large bust of Sun Yat-sen and various small artifacts.

Marco Polo Bridge

If bridges and their history are important to you then you will no doubt make the fifteen kilometre trip to the south west suburbs of Beijing to see the bridge which so pleased Marco Polo and which was the site of an incident that started the Sino-Japanese conflict in 1937.

Ivory Carver

A taxi will take you there or you can catch the bus to Zhujiafen alighting at Luguoqiao.

Marco Polo came across the bridge on a four-month trip, one of the many he made for Kublai Khan during his seventeen year stay at the imperial court. He was struck by the design of the bridge and immediately likened it to the great bridges of the world as he knew it.

This was during the 13th. century and he was looking at a bridge already a hundred years old and which was to stand unscathed, with the exception of minor alterations, until floods washed away two of the arches in 1698. That it lasted so long in a river notorious for its erratic currents and floods is a tribute to the engineering and building skills of the Jin dynasty architects who constructed the Lugouqiao (to give it its correct title) in 1192. The river was known as the **Lacking Stability River,** which says it all.

Eleven spans make up the bridge with 280 separate balusters supporting the balustrades. These balusters are responsible for the feature which is the main attraction of the bridge. Each baluster is individually carved with lions and their cubs all in varying positions. There are so many that they gave rise to a local saying: 'as uncountable as the lions on Lugou Bridge.' You can try counting them for yourself but the eyes become so confused at the interwoven patterns it is very easy to lose count. The official tally is 485 – but then, who's counting?

Yangtze River

However the major significance of the bridge is its location. This is where the Sino-Japanese war was launched.

In an incident, reminiscent of the infamous Polish 'attack' which Hitler stooged to justify his invasion of Poland, the Japanese invaded a nearby rail siding. Shots were fired between the Chinese and the marauders, and Japan then used the episode as an excuse for all-out war.

The bridge was widened during the 1950's to cope with growing post-war traffic but still retained its ancient appeal. Thankfully the authorities decided to build an additional bridge to handle modern transport needs. Upstream is the rail bridge of the main Beijing-Guangzhou (Canton) line. Suburbia may have overtaken the region and the addition of the steel mill is not a bonus but the bridge still has that indefinable 'presence'.

Cave of Peking Man

This, the last of the major sights of Beijing's outer districts, has a couple of unusual aspects.

For a start, in line with the revised spelling of the capital's name, this should be the cave of 'Beijing Man', but as it is universally known throughout the scientific world as 'Peking Man' it is proposed to stay with the latter title.

Then there is the question of the discoverer of our ancient friend.

The Chinese naturally give the honour to their own, the anthropologist Pei Wenzhong. Other authorities, foreign of course, claim it was the remarkable priest, philosopher and amateur archaeologist Fr. Teilhard de Chardin. Both were there so it can be

likened to the case of who actually made the first step onto Everest.

The important thing was the unearthing of the skullcap of the 500,000 year-old Peking Man on December 2nd. 1929, by a combined team of foreign and Chinese archaeologists.

Still if people are going to quibble we should give the kudos to those who, albeit unwittingly, first unearthed the ancient bones. These were local villagers from the tiny town of Zhoukoudian, 50 kilometres south-west of Beijing. Several years earlier they dug up some bones whilst fossicking in a quarry. With admirable shrewdness, if somewhat naively, they tried to pass them off for sale as the bones of dragons. Someone was curious enough to investigate further and before you could say 'St. George' the so-called 'dragon bones' were identified as being pre-historic and the race was on.

The other aspect, and the tragic one at that, is the disappearance of all the major fragments. During the confusion of World War 11 and its aftermath selfish interests spirited the Peking Man away. The blame is variously apportioned between the Japanese, the Americans and the Nationalist Chinese who fled to Taiwan. Eventually, when the illegal owners die, the treasures will no doubt surface. Some further pieces have been found since but not to the extent of the original dig.

The cave where the men of pre-history lived can be seen on the northern slopes of the appropriately named **Dragon Bone Hill** with further caves being the abodes of the more recent Homo Sapiens of a mere 18,000 years ago. The exhibition halls have some excellent fossilised remains of fish and animals but in general most are re-creations to show how the original skull would have looked and to depict the lifestyle of our early ancestors. From that point of view the trip is interesting if tinged with a little disappointment.

PART III
Accommodation

HOTELS

General Notes

Here is a comprehensive – but far from complete – list of the more recognised accommodation in the Beijing area.

> **INFOTIP:** The phone system works but ringing a local number is best done by someone speaking the language unless it is to a foreign firm based in Beijing. International calls can come through surprisingly quickly; at other times the patience of Confucius is required.

Legend

rm	rooms
AC	air-conditioning
Tel	rooms with telephone
TV	rooms with television
PB	rooms with private bathroom
R	restaurant
B	bar
C	coffee shop
S24	24-hour room service
P	babysitting
FE	foreign exchange
ReF	refrigeration in rooms
NC	night club
SP	swimming pool

BEIJING

Beiwei Hotel
Xi Jing Road, Xuan Wu District
Tel. 338631
The Beiwei Hotel has postal facilities and is located in the southern area of the city, approximately six kilometres from the railway station.

rm-176 AC Tel TV PB R FE

Capital Airport Guest House
Next to Capital Airport **Tel.** 555177
The Airport Guest House is conveniently situated less than a kilometre from the international terminal and offers postal facilities.

rm-210 AC Tel TV PB R FE

Beijing Hotel
21 East Chang'an Street **Tel.** 22426
This hotel is located in the heart of Beijing and provides its guests with postal services.

rm-901 AC Tel TV PB R B C FE

Bamboo Garden Hotel
24 Xiao Shi Qiao, Jiu Gu Lou Street
Tel. 444661
This hotel is located in the southern area of Beijing and features Chinese and Western restaurants and a Chinese garden.

rm-46 AC Tel TV PB R FE

Lido Hotel
Jichang Road **Tel.** 5006688
The Lido Hotel has health, postal
and sporting facilities and a shopping centre.

rm-484 AC Tel TV PB R B C P

Lüsongyuan Guest House
22 Jiao Dao Kou, Ban Chang Alley
This tiny guest house is centrally
located.

rm-21 AC PB R

Minzu Hotel
51 Fuxingmenwai Street
Tel. 658541
The Minzu Hotel has Chinese and
Western restaurants, a souvenir
shop and postal facilities. It is
located in central Beijing.

rm-607 AC Tel TV PB R B C FE

Heping Hotel
3 Jinyu Alley, Eastern City District
Tel. 558841
The Heping Hotel is located in central Beijing and has postal facilities
and a souvenir shop.

rm-114 AC Tel TV PB R B C FE

Hua Du Hotel
8 South Xin Yuan Road
Tel. 5001166
The Hua Du Hotel has postal services and souvenir and barber shops
and is located in eastern Beijing, not
far from the city centre.

rm-522 AC Tel TV PB R B C FE

Huilongguan Hotel
Chang Ping Road **Tel.** 275376
A small hotel in suburban Beijing.

rm-86 AC PB R C FE

Jianguo Hotel
3 Jianguomenwai Street
Tel. 5002233
Located in central Beijing, this hotel
has Chinese, Japanese and Western restaurants.

rm-454 AC Tel TV PB R B C P

Jinglun Hotel
Jianguomenwai Street
Tel. 5002266
This centrally located hotel has its
own shopping centre as well as con-
ference facilities and a health club.

rm-657 AC Tel TV PB R B C P

Overseas Chinese Hotel
5 Bei Xin Qiao San Taio **Tel.** 446611
The Overseas Chinese Hotel has a
shopping arcade and is located close
to the city centre.

rm-162 AC Tel TV PB R

Overseas Chinese Mansion
2 Wang Fu Jing Street **Tel.** 558851
This hotel is situated in central Beijing. Some rooms have air-condition-
ing, television and telephone. Suites
and some double bedrooms have
private baths.

rm-183 R FE

Qianmen Hotel
175 Yongan Road **Tel.** 338731
Located close to the city, the Qianmen has a souvenir shop and postal
facilities.

rm-389 AC Tel TV PB R B FE

Ti Yu Hotel
10 Tian Tan Road **Tel.** 752831
Situated close to central Beijing, The
Ti Yu Hotel offers both Chinese and
Western restaurants.

rm-8 AC Tel TV PB R

Olympic Hotel
52 Baishiqiao, Haidan District

rm-338 AC TV Ref Tel FE

The Great Wall Hotel, Beijing
A6 Donghuan Beilu **Tel.** 5005566
The Great Wall Hotel offers its
guests a full range of amenities
including a health club, shops and
conference facilities. The hotel can
also arrange sightseeing tours.

rm-982 AC Tel TV PB R C S24 FE

Fragrant Hill Hotel
Fragrant Hill Park, Haidian District
Tel. 285491
Located in suburban Beijing, the
Fragrant Hill Hotel has both Chinese
and Western restaurants as well as
postal facilities.

rm-292 AC Tel TV PB R B C P FE

Friendship Hotel
3 Hai Dian Road **Tel.** 890621
The Friendship Hotel has tennis
courts and postal and conference
facilities. It is located in western
Beijing.

rm-1339 AC Tel TV PB R B C P FE

Xinqiao Hotel
2 Dongjiaominxiang **Tel.** 557731
The Xinqiao Hotel is situated in the city centre within walking distance of the railway station.

rm-320 AC Tel TV PB R B FE

Xi Yuan Hotel
Erligou **Tel.** 890721
Located near the city centre the Xi Yuan Hotel has shops; Japanese, Chinese and Western restaurants; a health centre and postal facilities.

rm-711 AC Tel TV PB R B C P FE

Yanjing Hotel
19 Fuxingmenwai Street
Tel. 868721
Close to the city, the Yanjing Hotel has a barber shop and postal facilities.

rm-499 AC Tel TV PB R B C FE

Zhao Long Hotel
2 Northern Gongti Road, Chaoyang District **Tel.** 5002299
The Zhao Long Hotel has its own shopping centre and is located in inner Beijing.

rm-258 AC Tel TV PB R B C P FE

China World Hotel
1 Jian Guo Men Avenue
Tel. 594538
A superb new hotel and trade centre in the heart of Beijing.

rm-1051 AC Tel TV PB R B C S24 P FE Ref NC Sp

Furong Hotel
Balizhuang, Chaoyang District
Tel. 592921
Located 30 km from the Capital Airport and 7 km from the Beijing Railway Station.

rm-200 AC Tel TV FE R

Yanxiang Hotel
2 Jiang Tai Road **Tel.** 5006666
The Yanxiang Hotel is situated close to the airport.

rm-330 AC Tel TV PB R B C P FE

Taoran Hotel
Taipan Street, Taoranting Park
Taoran hotel is inside the Taoranting Park 5 km south of the Gate of Heavenly Peace. In the summer boating and fishing are available in the lake while in the winter there is skating and beautiful snow scenes from the park.

rm-145 AC TV Tel R

The Park Hotel
36 Pu Huang Yu Lu **Tel.** 7212233
Located at the southern part of Beijing, a few minutes drive to the Temple of Heaven.

TV R Tel

Wanshou Guest House
12A Wanshou Road **Tel.** 812901
This is a garden style hotel standing in quiet and secluded surroundings with an exuberant growth of trees.

rm-115 Tel TV Ref AC R FE

PART IV
Practical Information

PRACTICAL INFORMATION

A-Z Summary

Advance Planning

When to visit

Beijing is at its best during Autumn and Spring when the average maximum temperature is 21°C (70°F).

In the Summer it becomes extremely hot and humid with temperatures as high as 38°C (100°F), Beijing has a rainy season between July and August. China is better being avoided during Summer. The Winters are very cold and if you travel further north it gets colder still, the wind is biting and the average maximum temperature between December and March is −5°C (23°F) the average maximum is 0°C (32°F).

What to bring

Documents: passport, insurance cards, credit cards; you will be issued with Foreign Exchange Certificates on arrival in China.

Clothing: Being a tourist in Beijing can be hard work so it is important that you dress comfortably and practically. Unless you have a business meeting or a formal function planned in Beijing bring only comfortable, casual clothes.

Whatever season you visit Beijing in you will need sturdy comfort comfortable walking shoes or boots as tourists invariably do a lot of walking.

If you plan to be travelling about China and Beijing is just one stopping point you may be travelling through several different zones (except in summer when its hot everywhere). Try and pack clothes which you can wear in layers which can be taken off or added to as the weather allows as the Chinese are fairly strict about baggage allowances (20 kg).

Remember when you are packing to avoid bringing any revealing clothing which will attract some disapproval and a lot of attention.

Odds and Ends: Some western goods are available from Friendship Stores in Beijing but to be on the safe side it is probably best to bring your own sunscreen, shampoo, laundry powder, batteries, camera film, tooth paste and contact lens solutions.

Many brands of western cigarettes are available in China at reasonable prices but if you are very particular it may be a good idea to bring your own cigarettes with you.

Coffee again is something which is available in China, but not always exactly when you want it. If you like regular cups of coffee throughout the day you should bring your own instant coffee, sugar and long-life or powdered milk with you.

If Chinese tea is not to your taste it is also a good idea to bring your own tea with you to China.

Medical Tips: Travel insurance is a good idea when you are travelling to China as the costs of hospitalisation are high.

Bring your own medicines for throat, stomach and headaches with you to China as these types of medicines are often unavailable.

If you are taking any kind of medication make sure that you bring enough with you to last throughout your stay in China.

People with hearing aids should bring an adequate supply of batteries with them.

If you plan on travelling to rural areas of China in Spring or Summer a course of anti-malaria tablets is recommended.

Immunisation certificates are required by tourists who have passed through areas infected with yellow fever in the six days prior to their arrival in China.

Before you leave for China it is recommended that you visit your doctor for current information on immunisations.

> **INFOTIP:** Medical treatment for foreigners is normally done at a hospital unless the hotel has an 'on-call' doctor. Although the hospitals are far from glamorous they are functional and usually equipped with the latest drugs and equipment. The Capitol Hospital is noted for its treatment of glaucoma and related eye diseases.

Entry Regulations

To travel to China you must have a visa and a passport which will be valid for the duration of your stay in China. To obtain a visa contact the Chinese Consulate in your own country or a branch of the China International Travel Service (CITS – see 'Tourist Services').

If you are travelling to China as part of a tour group your travel agent will organise a group for all the group members to travel on.

> **INFOTIP:** Your visa for China is normally for three months and dates from the time of issue so if undertaking a lengthy trip prior to entering China then check that the visa will still be valid upon arrival otherwise you are likely to be turned away at the airport.

Customs

When entering China you will be asked to fill in a customs declaration form on which you list all items such as cameras, electronic goods, watches or jewellery which you are bringing into China with you. Remember to declare any gifts which you bring with you. You must keep the carbon copy of your declaration form with you until you leave China as customs officials may ask you to prove that you are in fact taking all items listed on the form with you from China.

You are permitted to bring up to 400 cigarettes, 2 bottles of alcoholic beverages not exceeding 3/4 and up to 6 dozen rolls of camera film with you to China.

You are not permitted to bring explosives, firearms, Chinese currency, pornographic material, addictive drugs or radio transmitting equipment with you to China.

Currency

You may not bring Chinese currency with you into China, though bringing in foreign currency is permitted. There is no limit to the amount of foreign currency you can bring into China.

When leaving China you may take with you Foreign Exchange Certificates (tourist money) but not Renminbi (RMB).

> **INFOTIP:** Keep all your exchange receipts from changing foreign currency to Chinese with you as you may have to produce these before any-excess currency certificates you have will be changed back to foreign currency when you leave China.

Getting To Beijing

By air: Many major airlines offer flights to Beijing. There are direct flights between Beijing and the major cities of Europe, Asia, the United States and Australia. There are also regular flights between Hongkong and Beijing and a variety of domestic flights from within China.

By rail: Train services to Beijing from all over China are regular and efficient. Bearing in mind that train travel is time consuming it is also a wonderful way to see more of China. Travelling 'soft class' on Chinese trains is quite comfortable and express services and sleepers are available.

Electricity

Voltage differs in each area of China so try not to bring too many electrical appliances with you – and bring adaptor plugs for any appliances you do bring.

Voltage is usually 220-240 V and plugs usually have two either round or flat pins.

Entertainment

Children's Entertainment

There are a few parks in Beijing but children should be kept amused by any sightseeing that you do. They will especially enjoy the acrobatic and puppet shows which are given around Beijing.

One thing children enjoy is the Beijing Zoo in Xishen Street in north-west Beijing. It is China's biggest zoo and features both domestic and exotic animals. A visit to this zoo can however be quite depressing for adults as the animals have only a little space to move around in.

Situated near the zoo is the Beijing planetarium.

Babysitting

Tourists do not usually bring their children with them to China, so most hotels will not have babysitting facilities. If a babysitter is required you can always try asking hotel staff to see if something can be arranged.

Cinema

The International Club in Beijing sometimes shows Chinese films with English subtitles.

Dance

European and Chinese ballets are both performed in Beijing. Both are of a high standard but for tourists the Chinese dance may be more interesting. The ballets are often based upon tales of ancient China.

Cultural shows

Featuring the songs and dances of China's various ethnic groups are also very entertaining. These shows are usually brief and move quickly from one national group to the next so there is no time to get bored. The costumes of the different groups are especially interesting.

Music

The works of European composers are popular in China and though concerts are not quite up to international standards they are highly entertaining.

Operas

Chinese operas are dramatic performances that tourists either love or loathe. They have all the ingredients necessary to move the plot along – wicked villains, bold heros and fair damsels – but props are kept down to a bare minimum and mime is used extensively and so people who do not speak Chinese are often left confused and bored by the whole experience. If you have a guide who can translate for you you will enjoy the opera much much more.

Even if you do not have a guide to explain things to you Chinese opera can still be enjoyed. The costumes are magnificent and performers wear elaborate masks, with spectacularly malevolent creations being donned by the actors who play the villains. Acrobats also appear in the opera and liven things up.

You may find that on a group tour your group will be edged out of the theatre shortly after the performance has begun. This is as your guide will probably expect that westerners will not enjoy the opera. If you ask your guide if you can arrange to see an entire opera they will probably be happy to oblige.

Shadow Puppets

Shadow puppeteers have been enchanting audiences in China for over two thousand years.

The puppeteer moves flat puppets behind a white silk screen whilst a bright light causes a shadow to be cast on the screen in the shape of the puppet. The puppeteers also provide voices for their creations which can be made to sing or dance as the story requires.

Ancient legends are a popular basis for shadow puppet plays and you will find both professional and amateur groups giving performances. The plays might sound like something for children but adults enjoy them too so don't miss out on a chance to see a shadow puppet play.

Acrobats

Acrobatic performances featuring jugglers, comedians, trapeze artists, contortionists and magicians are often given for tourist groups and are really very enjoyable. Chinese acrobats train to a very high standard and, like the shadow puppets, their shows are for adults as well as children.

Festivals and National Holidays

Spring Festival or Chinese New Year

The Spring Festival is a Three day holiday celebrating the new year. During this festival the Chinese like to buy new clothes, settle debts, exchange gifts and enjoy rich food.

The **Lantern Festival** marks the end of the Spring Festival in a noisy, colourful celebration.

Qingming

The Qingming festival honours the dead and this is the traditional time for the Chinese to visit and tend to the graves of their ancestors.

Dragon Boat Festival

The Dragon Boat Festival commemorates the death of the ancient poet Qu Yuan drowned in the Hunan province. The Dragon Boats in the festival symbolise the boats that raced to save Qu Yuan but were too late.

Rice cakes with nut and date centres are traditionally eaten during this festival.

Mid Autumn Festival

During this festival people look forward to a plentiful harvest and watch the full moon. Cakes made from dates, sesame and lotus seeds are eaten during the Mid Autumn Festival.

> **INFOTIP:** The dates of these festivals are determined by the Chinese lunar calendar and so fall on different days each year. Ask your travel agent before you leave for China about current dates for Chinese festivals.

National Holidays

January 1	**New Years Day**
January or February	**Spring Festival (Chinese New Year)**
May 1	**Labour Day**
October 1	**National Day**

Getting Around in Beijing

Public Transport

Public transport is certainly the cheapest way to get around Beijing but it is not the easiest. Firstly all public transport guides and maps are only available in Chinese, so you could have trouble finding your way about and secondly buses and trains are very very crowded so travelling on them is certainly not a pleasant experience.

Buses

Beijing's bus routes can take you past some of the city's premier tourist attractions if you are confident enough to get on board.

The first problem for people who don't speak Chinese is paying the fare. Fares are calculated on distance so you must be able to name your destination in Chinese when you get on the bus. One way to get around this is to have someone at your hotel write down your destination in Chinese and you can show this to the driver. Make sure you have the name of your hotel also written down so you can find your way home.

The second problem is fighting your way on and off the buses which always seem to be crowded.

Metro

Beijing's underground railway system is easier to acquaint yourself with than the bus system – mainly because station names are written on signs at the stations in pinyin.

These trains are still crowded though and in rush hour they are really only for the strong and thrifty.

Bicycle

There are over three million cyclists in Beijing and biking is a fun way to see more of the city.

Bikes can be hired (there is a shop opposite the Friendship Store) and you may have to leave a deposit or your passport when you take a bicycle.

Beijing is very flat so cycling is easy but you should be aware that bicycles are not permitted on some streets and that the traffic is chaotic and can be dangerous.

Taxi

Travelling by taxi is an inexpensive and convenient way to get around Beijing. Taxis don't wait at stands or cruise the streets looking for customers in Beijing but they can easily be arranged and most hotels, shops and restaurants will call a taxi for you.

Taxi drivers do not accept tips and will give change to the exact amount.

If you are planning on sightseeing around Beijing and want to get from place to place easily then consider hiring a taxi for a day or for a few hours. It doesn't cost very much and it means that you won't have to waste time getting about.

Tour Bus

CITS tour buses in China can be gloriously modern or ricketty unsprung horrors in which you freeze in winter and suffocate in summer. Luckily for tourists most tour buses are modern so you can sightsee in comfort.

Getting Out of Beijing

By air: Beijing's Capital Airport is situated about 40 minutes drive from the city and can be reached by bus or taxi.

For flight enquiries tel: 552515   555531X382

Major airlines with offices in Beijing
AEROFLOT tel: 522181
AIR FRANCE tel: 523487
CAAC tel: 558861
ETHIOPIAN AIRLINES tel: 523285
IRANAIR tel: 523249
JAPAN AIRLINES tel: 523457
LUFTHANSA tel: 522626
PHILIPPINE AIR LINES tel: 522794
QANTAS tel: 5002481
SWISSAIR tel: 523284
UNITED AIRLINES tel: 5001985

By rail: Travel by rail may be time consuming, but it is a fantastic way to see more of China. Foreigners usually travel 'soft class' and so can watch the scenery in comfort. 'Hard class' is less comfortable and more crowded.

The railway service in China is efficient and trains usually run on time and express services and sleepers are available.

At Beijing station in Jianguomenwai Avenue a seperate waiting room is provided for foreigners away from the rush and crowd. Inquiries: tel: 554866.

Motoring

There are no self-drive rental cars available in Beijing as the traffic, roads and road signs are just too much for the average tourist to cope with. You can however easily hire a chauffeur driven car. Ask at your hotel desk for particulars of car-hire companies or ask your CITS guide and they should be able to arrange something for you. If you only want a car for a few hours then you can always hire a taxi at an hourly rate.

> **INFOTIP:** Driving yourself is not recommended for the impatient. The roads in Beijing are crowded with cyclists whose lack of road sense is a wonder to behold. There is no system of petrol stations as in the West. Petrol for hire cares is distributed through special government-controlled depots and as these are not clearly marked it is wise to get a map pinpointing the depots before you set out.

Photography

Most types of camera film are available in the Friendship Store in Beijing, but to be on the safe side you might like to pack a good supply of film. You can get your film processed in China, but most people prefer to wait until they get home to have their films developed.

One thing to remember in China is not to take pictures of individual people without first getting their permission.

Post Offices

Most hotels have small post offices or a postal service desk where you can buy postcards, stamps and writing paper. These are usually open from 8am until 6pm from Mondays to Saturdays and from 8am until 12noon on Sundays.

Mail leaving China generally travels slowly. Surface mail takes a few months to arrive overseas and even airmail letters take about ten days.

Post restante: Chinese post offices do not have post restante facilities.

Philately: Philatelic products can be brought in post offices, at the postal desks in hotels and at the China Stamp Exporting Company at 28 Donghuamen Jie.

Publications in English

You can find a surprising number of English language publications available from newsstands in Beijing's major hotels. There is the Asian Wall Street Journal, the International Herald Tribune, the China Daily, the China Pictorial and the Beijing Review; as well as Time and Newsweek.

Books in English can often be bought in hotels as well as tourist books and translations of Chinese novels.

Maps

Free maps are available at hotels and tourist attractions and they are designed to help tourists find their way to various sightseeing spots.

Maps are also for sale at newsstands and bookshops which give more detailed street plans if you want to wander off the tourist trail.

Religious Services

Ask at your hotel desk for information about religious services. If you are in a tour group tell your guide of you intention or attending church so that you can make time for this in your schedule.

Help!

Embassies

Services provided by your Embassy are listed below. These services exist by agreement with the host countries and are bound by certain local regulations, as well as by orders from their home countries.

Questions regarding:.
– Visas and passports
– Difficulties with local regulations (Customs, the law, etc.)
– Assistance with absentee voting in home country
– Notarisation or witnessing of documents
– Assistance in case of death
– Embassies are supposed to be notified in case of hospitalisation of a foreigner, if the nationality of the patient is known.
– You should contact your Embassy if you are involved in any type of accident whilst you are in China.
– In case of arrest your Embassy should be notified.

Australia 15 Dongzhimenwai St., Sanlitun; tel: 522331
Britain 22 Kuanghua Rd., Jianguomenwai; tel: 521961
Canada 10 Sanlitun Rd., Chao Yang District; tel: 521475, 521571, 521724
France 3 Sanlitun Rd., Chao Yang District; tel: 521331, 521332
Democratic Republic of Germany
Federal Republic of Germany 5 Dong Zhimen Wai St., Chao Yang District; tel: 522161
Japan 7 Ritan Rd., Jianguomenwai; tel: 522361
New Zealand 2 Ritan Donger St., Chao Yang District; tel: 522731
Philippines 23 Hsiu Shui Pie St., Jianguomenwai; tel: 522794
Poland tel: 521235
Switzerland 3 Dongwu St., tel: 522831

United States 17 Guanghua Rd.; tel: 522033
U.S.S.R tel: 521267

Medical Emergency telephones Beijing

Ambulance 555678
Shoudu/Xiehe Hospital 553731
Beijing Friendship Hospital 338671

Police Emergencies

Beijing is a fairly safe city and there is comparatively little crime. You should however watch out for pick-pockets and it is not a good idea to leave bags unattended. If you suspect that something has been stolen report it immediately to your guide, hotel desk or to the police.

The police in China wear green uniforms with caps bearing the Chinese insignia. The uniform of the Chinese airforce is unfortunately very similar. In case of doubt the word for police is jingchá.
Police: tel: 550720

Death

The death of a foreign citizen requires immediate consultation with his/her embassy by friends, relatives, hospital or police authorities.

Lost Property

Items lost by foreigners are usually easily identifiable in China so lost property should not be too much of a problem.

If you lose anything, or suspect that something has been stolen, report the loss/theft to the CITS office, to your guide or to hotel staff.

The loss or theft of passports or other important documents should be reported to your embassy.

Replacement of certain items

Airline tickets: Report the loss/theft to the airline and request another ticket. Some proof of purchase may be needed before a replacement ticket will be issued.

Restaurants

Dining out in Beijing can be a lot of fun but it's not the easy, casual affair it is in the West. The lack of Western-style restaurants (with the exception of those in the major hotels) is the main stumbling block for those looking for something other than Chinese food. However the gourmet who appreciates the subtleties of Chinese cooking with all its regional differences and delicacies will find a good range of well-run restaurants catering for a wide spectrum of tastes.

With the restaurants listed here it is wise to book using your guide or concierge to facilitate the language problem on the phone. These restaurants are considered to be the best and do understand Western needs. There are hundreds of smaller restaurants scattered throughout Beijing and if you are feeling adventurous you can sample these. However standards of hygiene in the smaller establishments are variable and, unless you strike a student learning the language, English is not understood so you will have to order by pointing at a neighbour's dish that looks interesting. Remember the Chinese eat early and by 9pm most restaurants are empty. There is no lingering over coffee; as soon as the last course is eaten they quickly depart.

For convenience the restaurants are listed by regional cuisine.

Beijing

Because the climate here in the north tends to be cooler there is a tendency to a spicier form of cooking. The city is famous for its Beijing Duck (or Peking Duck) and it is a standard ritual for foreign tourists to be taken to one of the several major restaurants specialising in this dish. In fact the restaurants generally serve only dishes made from parts or products of the duck e.g. Duck Soup, Pickled Duck's Feet, Duck Eggs, Duck Liver, etc. The main course is the famous Roast Duck which, if correctly done, involves force feeding, the pumping of air under the skin and a slow roasting over wood fires. It is always served in small spices accompanied with tiny 'pancakes', spring onions and plum sauce.

Peking Roast Duck Restaurant (24 Qianmen St. Tel. 751379): one of Beijing's oldest being opened in 1864. It is called the 'Big Duck' to distinguish it from a sister establishment. Its maze of rooms are always crowded with foreigners normally separated from the locals who enjoy a cheaper menu.

Peking Roast Duck Restaurant (13 Shuaifuyuan St. Tel. 553310); a companion operation to the above and known as the 'Side Duck' which is not a reflection on the cooking but because of its location near the Capitol Hospital close by Beijing Hotel.

Sichuan

Sichuan cooking is the spiciest in China. A liberal use of chillies, peppers and garlic will play havoc with the ulcers and the breath but the food is delicious if unsubtle.

E Mei (cnr. Lishi Rd & Yuetan Nth. St. Tel. 863068): the name comes from a famous mountain in Sichuan Province. Popular with locals and cheap.

Sichuan (51 Rong Xian. Tel. 336356). Considered to be the best of this region's restaurants. Expensive although there are cheaper back rooms with a more limited menu. The food is guaranteed to leave you gasping for water.

Cantonese

Ostensibly blander when compared with other styles this is better known to Westerners due to the ubiquitous Cantonese fast-food outlets that flourish on all continents. However when practised carefully Cantonese cooking can reveal subtle flavours that the spiciness of other regional cuisines cover up.

Guangdong Canting (Xijao Shichang near the Zoo. Tel. 894881): features sweet and sour pork, turtle, snake, bamboo shoots and fillets of canine (!).

Mongolian

The hardy Mongols who inhabit the windswept plains of Mongolia rely heavily on hearty cooking heavy on fatty lamb and with no worries about fancy trimmings. The main feature of their cuisine is the Mongolian Hot Pot, a variation on the fondue with strips of lamb being cooked at the table in a pot of boiling water to which is added vegetables and spices to form the soup with which the meal ends. In Mongolia itself it is customary to hack away at lamb bones using just a single knife and one's hands. Messy but fun; however Beijing's restaurateurs are usually more refined. The Mongolian Hot Pot is often served only in winter.

Donglaishun (16 Jinyu Hutung Tel. 550069): renowned for its Mongolian Hot Pot which it serves year-round. Was also known as the 'Nationalities Restaurant' and is part of a 5-restaurant complex in the East Wind Market just north of the Beijing Hotel.

National Minorities Restaurant (Fuxingmen Avenue Tel. 660544): not to be confused with the above restaurant this is part of the Palace of the National Minorities and a booking would be required. Like most restaurants serving Mongolian food this also caters for the large Muslim community.

Western and other Cuisines

Beijing Sucui Canting (74 Xuanwumennai St. Tel. 334296): a vegetarian restaurant which offers chicken, fish and beef dishes in which only vegetables, nuts, beancurd and spices are used. Clever and tasty camouflage.

Maxim's (2 Qianmendong Ave. Tel. 754003). Beijing's fanciest eating house with fancy prices. A branch of the famed Paris establishment. French cooking and, after initial mishaps, service to match.

Moscow Restaurant (Beijing Exhibition Centre Tel. 893713): opposite the zoo this is part of the Exhibition complex built by the Russians who erected a church-like steeple on top which has become a local landmark. The menu features borscht, stroganoff, caviar and other comradely fare.

Kentucky Fried chicken (Qianmen St): it may be a case of 'taking coals to Newcastle' but this 500-seater fast food outlet handily situated by Tian'anmen Square is a big drawcard for the locals and those Westerners suffering withdrawal symptoms without their daily 'fix' of the good Colonel's cooking.

Shopping

You should have many opportunities to shop in Beijing, and even guided tours include shopping trips. Although tacky souvenirs can certainly be found in China you can also pick up some real bargains as prices in China tend to be much lower than they are in the west. The following descriptions may help you with your shopping.

Antiques: The export of antiques is strictly controlled in China. Only objects marked with a special wax seal can be taken out of the country, and these are all under 120 years old.

Bargains are also unlikely when buying antiques in Beijing as dealers, and only a few are licensed to sell to foreigners, know exactly the value of the goods found in their shops.

However, you can look even if you can't buy and antique shops make wonderful sightseeing.

Bamboo Products: You will find all sorts of things made from bamboo in Beijing, from delicate chopsticks and fans to furniture.

Bronzeware: Bronze vases, bowls and plates can be bought cheaply in Beijing, and many of these are engraved in extravagant designs.

Carpets and Rugs: Wool or silk oriental rugs are popular tourist buys. Shop around a little before you buy to get the best price, and if possible buy from a large store which can arrange shipping.

Chops: Chops or seals are used by the Chinese instead of written signatures. They are made from ivory, jade, plastic or stone and have the characters which form a name carved on their base. By pressing the base into ink and then onto a sheet of paper you produce an instant signature. You can have your own name carved onto a chop in Chinese characters for a unique souvenir.

Chopsticks: You can buy all kinds of chopsticks in Beijing. Choose from a range of plain chopsticks or try the gorgeously painted chopsticks which come in their own little boxes. Chopsticks are practical souvenirs if you plan to be cooking and eating Chinese food when you get back home. The longer, thicker chopsticks are used for cooking.

Cloissoné: Chinese cloissoné is of a very high standard and is used on a variety of objects. Enamelware jewellery, plates and vases are all good buys.

Fabrics: China's silks and cottons are of exceptional quality and are also inexpensive. You can choose from a wide variety of colours and prints and buy the fabric by the metre or already made up into blouses, scarfs and dresses.

Fans: Millions of fans are produced in China each year. Many are mass-produced and 'cheap and nasty' but you will also find beautifully made wooden and paper fans.

Figurines: Colourful, quaint figurines of animals or historic or legendary figures are popular in China and can be bought from shops or souvenir stalls.

Furniture: When buying furniture in Beijing look out for quality in the materials used in the work. Carved wooden furniture is an especially evocative reminder of China. When buying furniture it is best to buy from a store which can arrange shipping.

Ginseng: Ginseng is famed in China for its medicinal properties, and you might like to try it for yourself. The best ginseng tends to be expensive, but remember that it can be bought more cheaply in Beijing than in the herbalist stores in Hongkong.

Herbs and Spices: Look for spice stalls in the markets, they stock a bewildering array of exotic herbs and seasonings; some of which can only be found in certain regions of China. If you want to take any of these spices home check your country's import regulations first as many nations restrict the importation of plant products.

Kites: Beijing can be quite windy so you will find a variety of kites available there. The kites can be very simple or very elaborate in their design and they make wonderful take home gifts for children.

Lacquerware: Lacquerware plates, cups, trays and boxes make attractive and practical souvenirs — especially if you enjoy Chinese food. If you develop a taste for Chinese tea look out for beautiful lacquerware tea services.

Luggage: Inexpensive suitcases and bags are good buys in Beijing if you are facing the problem of having bought more than will fit in your own bags in China.

Musical Instruments: You can buy both Chinese and Western instruments in Beijing at very good prices.

Paintings: Both original paintings and hand-drawn copies of ancient paintings can be bought in Beijing. These come in scrolls and are very good as souvenirs and gifts.

Papercuts: Papercuts are delicate pieces of artwork made with scissors. They make decorative souvenirs.

Porcelain: Porcelain in China is described as being first, second or third class. The Chinese numerals for one, two and three are printed on the price tag so you can be sure of the quality of porcelain you are buying.

Reproductions: In Beijing there are available many reproductions of museum pieces and archeological treasures. These can be bought from shops, souvenir stalls or museums.

Rubbings: Stone rubbings taken from temples or ancient carvings are popular souvenirs.

Souvenirs: Chinese dolls, clothing and posters — in short a whole range of souvenir items — can be found in stores and markets all over Beijing.

Tea: If you develop a fondness for Chinese teas you can buy a whole range to take home and enjoy. Make sure though that the teas are packaged in accordance with the customs regulations of your own country.

Toys: China produces many kinds of children's toys which are both inexpensive and durable.

Woollens: Chinese woollens are inexpensive and a good range of cashmere sweaters are also available in Beijing. The style of woollen clothing which can be found in Beijing is also improving so while you cannot expect anything too new and exciting you can pick up quality woollen scarves and jumpers at good prices.

Where to Shop

Friendship Stores: Friendship Stores came about as places where export goods could be sold to foreigners but they now also stock imported goods for the benefit of foreign residents of Beijing. Now for tourists convenience they also carry Chinese goods which are not intended for export — the type of thing you would find in any Chinese shop.

The advantages of shopping in a Friendship Store are that the staff will usually speak a little English and that you should be able to use your credit card in a Friendship Store. Friendship stores are also less crowded than the local stores and their wares are usually of good quality. A major advantage is that Friendship Store staff will arrange to have any large purchases crated and shipped home for you, and you can also change foreign currency at Friendship Stores.

Friendship Store disadvantages are the prices, while they may seem reasonable the same goods may be available elsewhere for much less. You also miss out on seeing how the locals shop in a Friendship store.

The Beijing Friendship Store is located in Jianguomenwai Avenue; tel: 593531.

Souvenir shops: Souvenir shops are scattered all over Beijing and sell a variety of souvenirs, some of which are mass-produced and awful and other which are of reasonable quality.

The best of the souvenir shops are found in handicraft factories and usually sell attractive and well-made goods.

Department Stores: You can buy a wide range of goods in Beijing's department stores, though don't expect quite the same range of luxury items as you would find in the west.

You may find that to buy some items, such as fabrics, in department stores you will need ration coupons. Your guide may be able to get these for you but this would be very difficult so try the Friendship Store first.

In Beijing try the department store at 255 Wangfujing avenue.

Free Markets: You can buy almost anything at a free market, including handicrafts, clothing jewellery and furniture.

Try the Beitaitingzhan or the Chaoyangmennei markets for bargain hunting.

Wangfujing Avenue: Beijing's best shopping street is Wangfujing Avenue. Here you will find the Beijing Department Store (tel: 556761), the Beijing Arts and Crafts Centre (tel: 556806) and many other local stores.

Liulichang: Liulichang is the area of Beijing people come to buy arts, crafts and antiques. Here you can buy porcelain, reproduction figures, bronzeware and a variety of antique goods — though the prices of these are high.

Shopping Hours: In Beijing Friendship Stores and department stores open from 9am until 7 or 8pm, seven days a week. Smaller, local shops occasionally stay open later.

Telephone and Telegraph

Local calls

Local calls can be made from public telephone booths or from your hotel room. The cost of making a local call from a coin-operated telephone is only a few fen.

Long Distance and Overseas Calls

Long distance or international calls have to be placed through an operator. These calls can be booked at your hotel and you can take the call at the hotel service desk or in your room. Hotels can arrange reverse charge calls.

Service Numbers
Information 114
Long-distance information 116
Overseas operator 337431
Domestic long-distance operator 330100 331230

USEFUL PHRASES: Where is the telephone?
Diàn-hug zài nǎr?

Time

In Beijing and all over China is GMT plus 8 hours.

Tipping

Tipping has now reached China. It is now customary to tip as you would in the West. As well as the national guide who accompanies you throughout China, your local guide should also be looked after as the world can easily be spread along the grapevine and the service you get in later cities may not be what you would expect.

Toilets

Toilets tend to be rather primitive in China, and worse is the lack of cubicle doors (or even cubicles). Always carry tissues and soap, as many public toilets do not have paper or soap.

Tourist Services

The China International Travel Service or Luxingshe looks after all tourists in China to some extent and it is through the CITS that tours are organised and accommodation arranged.

If you have any problems in China and would like to contact the CITS just ask your guide or your hotel desk for the nearest office.

Beijing: 6 Chang'an Dong Ave., tel: 551031
Shanghai: 33 Zhongshan Road E; tel: 324960

Overseas:
China Tourist Office, 4 Glenworth St., London NW1, England
Office Du Tourisme de Chine, 51 Rue Sainte-anne 75002, FRANCE
China Tourist Office, Eschenheimer Anlage 28, D-6000 Frankfurt am
Main-1, FEDERAL REPUBLIC OF GERMANY
China Tourist Office, 6F Hachidai Hamamatsucho B1. 1-27-13,
Hamatsu-cho, Minato-ku, Tokyo, JAPAN
China Tourist Office, Lincoln Building, 60 E. 42nd St., Suite 465,
New York, N.Y. 10165, U.S.A.

Water

Never drink water straight from the tap in China. The thermoses of
hot water left in hotel rooms for tea making are usually fairly safe, but
the cool 'drinking' water left in the rooms is better left untouched.

Sports and Athletics

Government policy is to encourage sport and the Chinese people
especially the young are quick to take advantage of any sporting
facility available.

Athletics and Gymnastics
Are basic school and university activities

Basketball
Very popular sport and in international matches China can field teams
of surprising height

Tennis or Ping Pong
This is the speciality of the Chinese. This social game has been turned
in China into one of skill, tactics and adroid athleticism.

Tai Ji Quan or Tai Chi
Tai Chi is attributed with keeping the body supple. Anywhere in China,
first thing in the morning you will see young and old going through
the intricate and slow routine.

Xiang Qi
Similar to Western game of Chess, dating from the eighth century
AD, is one game you will see played often.

Tiao Qi
Is played with marbles and a board with holes, we know it as Chinese
Checkers.

Mah Jong
This is a simple form of draughts very popular to pass the time.

PART V
Business Guide

BUSINESS GUIDE

General Notes

The business face of China has changed remarkably over the last few years and this is most noticeable in the area of tourism. Hard currency is being earned through tourism and a developing export programme of consumer goods.

At present, Beijing has 260 Sino-foreign joint ventures, cooperative enterprises and foreign investment enterprises, with direct foreign investment of US $1.6 billion. Companies, Banks and industrial enterprises from 41 countries and regions have set up almost 1000 offices in the city.

Changes in the international economy have provided China with new chances. Some developed countries and regions are readjusting their business structure and will move some high-cost labour enterprises to places with lower labour cost. China's coastal area is very attractive to them with its large supply of labour at low cost and a relatively high education. There are good energy resources, transportation and communication facilities and strong scientific technological possibilities.

The United States, Japan and the EEC countries are China's main suppliers of advanced technology. Cooperation with Russia and Eastern European countries in energy, transportation and communications has also grown in recent years. China is using French nuclear technology in the construction of the Guangdong Nuclear Power Station, British electricity generating techniques for China's oil fields and Italian petrochemical equipment in Liaoning province.

China has a great potential for technology export, thousands of scientific invations have been made by Chinese scientists in recent years.

New Technology Department Corporation has established agreements with a dozen companies in Britain, America and Japan to co-produce computer software.

It has also adopted flexible measures to facilitate the garment industry, for example since material for high class garments is insufficient some companies have begun processing garments using customers materials on a compensation trade basis.

Business Briefing

Main Industries: Textiles, toys, clothing small appliances.
Main agricultural products: rice, poultry, pork
Main Imports: Cereals, rolled steel, fertilisers, machinery, sugar, unprocessed cotton.
Main exports: Crude oil, refined petroleum products, textiles, clothing, canned goods, coal fruit and vegetables.
Principle trading partners: Hong Kong, Japan, USA, West Germany, Jordan, Canada

Exchange Import and Export of Currency

Chinese currency can not be taken out of China. There is no limit to the amount of foreign currency which may be brought into or taken out of China. Foreign Exchange Certificates which will be issued on arrival can be exchanged for foreign currency on departure.

Trade Fairs

A Trade Fair is held every April and October in Canton.

Banks

Chinese Banks

BANK OF CHINA 17 Xijiaomin Xiang; tel: 338521

Foreign Banks

NATIONAL AUSTRALIA BANK tel: 330193, 333147
WESTPAC BANKING CORPORATION tel: 595261 Ext 100

Banking Hours

Most hotels have foreign exchange offices which are open from 7.30 or 8am until 7pm, though the hours depend upon the size of the hotel. Larger hotels designed with western tourists in mind have foreign exchange offices which stay open later.

Credit Cards

American Express Room 1410, Beijing Hotel; tel: 552331

Translators and Interpreters

Easily available through the hotel reception, tour operator or your local guide.
    (See also Travel Service PART IV)

Convention Facilities

There is a huge number of convention facilities available in China. All major hotels cater for conventions. The newly open China World Trade Centre in Beijing not only has a convention and exhibition centre but also high and low class office blocks plus residential appartments.
    (See also Tourist Service PART IV)

Alphabetical Index

Index